I'll Walk With You

I'll Walk With You

A Journey of Believing

Geri Marshall

Outskirts Press, Inc.
Denver, Colorado

Outskirts Press, Inc.
http://www.outskirtspress.com

PB ISBN: 978-1-4327-3564-7
HB ISBN: 978-1-4327-3919-5

Library of Congress Control Number: 2009927887

Outskirts Press and the "OP" logo are trademarks belonging to Outskirts Press, Inc.

PRINTED IN THE UNITED STATES OF AMERICA

Prologue

I was nine years old when I first learned that Nissa would be entering my life. I had an older brother named Shane and two younger brothers, Wade and Garren. Our father called us together one night and announced, "There is going to be another little one around here come spring." It was unusual to be called together for an announcement, so it left an impression on me. I wasn't really sure what he was talking about either, so that may be another reason I remember the event.

I was 10 years old and in the fourth grade when she arrived. My Dad brought home a little black-and-white picture of her when he returned from the hospital. I remember her squished-up face kind of bothering me. I expected to see something more like the round-faced baby dolls I got for Christmas. Everyone was excited that I finally had a sister, and I was excited to share my bedroom with someone. But I didn't really know what it would be like to have a sister.

When she got big enough to stand up in her crib, she could reach my dresser. She liked pulling on the dresser scarf to see how it made everything go flying off the edge and onto the floor. She was always delighted with her accomplishments. I remember how cute she was when she was learning to walk.

She was a very sweet, feminine little girl. My Mom was excited to have a girl that acted like a girl. I was 100 percent tomboy; I loved climbing trees and playing outside with the boys. Nissa liked dresses and dolls and was very easygoing.

As I entered my teen years, I spent less time at home so I didn't have much interaction with my younger siblings. Nissa was only eight years old when I left home for college. She was always my cute, sweet little sister. I saw her during holidays and for a couple months at a time on summer breaks from college.

When Nissa was ten years old, and I twenty, we had another sister, Teena, join the family. People who didn't know my family usually assumed Teena was my child. It wasn't just because of the age difference; we both had blondish colored hair. I suppose it is odd to have one and two decades separating siblings, but we don't seem to notice. We are just who we are regardless of our ages. And for this chapter of our lives, we have the privilege of spending it together—time that I will always cherish.

I am married to a great guy named Tim and we have one son named Jesse. Jesse is now married to a beautiful young woman named Shaura, whom we feel honored to have in our clan.

Table of Contents

CHAPTER 1

I'll Walk With You

I had retired early for a Friday night. It was November 30, 2001 and I was fast asleep when the phone rang. The masculine voice on the other end of the line announced himself as a police officer. My mind immediately started down a check list: Was Jesse home? Was Tim on the road? Where is Teena? Was the dog barking? The only other time I had received a nighttime call from the police was to issue a "disturbing the peace" ticket from my dog barking and keeping a neighbor awake.

The checklist helped me struggle my way back to being awake. The officer gave me a moment before he continued. "Your sister has been taken to the emergency room in American Fork. She is alright but they would like you to come," he said in a matter-of-fact tone.

A series of questions immediately started marching across my waking mind: What was wrong? Was she in an accident? Was she really all right? Did he just say she was all right so I would not be too reactive? What I really wanted to know was why a police officer was calling. I eventually asked him, but his explanation didn't make sense to me so I thanked him and hung up the phone.

Teena lived with me at the time, so I got her out of bed and we headed across the valley to American Fork. Nissa's husband looked relieved to see us when we walked into the little curtained cubical in the emergency room. He announced our arrival to Nissa as if he hoped it would arouse her from wherever she had drifted off to, but she didn't move. She didn't open her eyes or nod her head or acknowledge our entrance in any way. Her lack of response concerned me.

"They think she has an ear infection," he said with a great deal of uncertainty in his voice. The ear infection theory did not match her non-responsive presentation, so I asked what had happened.

Nissa had been up nursing her one-month-old daughter, Carli. She suddenly felt nauseated so she set the baby down and headed for the bathroom. She almost made it to the toilet before she collapsed to the floor and began to vomit violently. She was unable to talk or move, and struggled to breath. When the ambulance arrived she was unable to get up off the floor. It was as if she had no control of her body at all.

"Have they ruled out a stroke?" I asked in a lowered voice as I stepped out of the little cubical. I didn't want Nissa to hear the question.

"The paramedic told me that he thought it was a stroke but the doctor doesn't think so," her husband said. There was a hint of discomfort in his voice.

"She couldn't even breathe when it first happened," he added in a distressed tone.

I didn't like the incongruence between how severe the symptoms had been and a minor diagnosis like an ear infection. I decided to try to talk to Nissa directly in hopes of getting some clarity.

Re-entering the cubical, I walked to Nissa's side, touched her arm, and attempted to get her attention with my voice. She continued to be unresponsive.

"How long has she been like this?" I asked. No one answered me.

The doctor decided to keep her in the hospital overnight because he was concerned about her being dehydrated. That didn't make any more sense to me than the ear infection theory but I was glad she was in the hospital. She was moved from the emergency room to a regular hospital room.

Teena went to Nissa's house to stay with the children and I stayed in Nissa's room watching every breath she took all night long. The words "she couldn't even breathe" haunted me as I kept watch.

About 6 a.m. a doctor came in to do his rounds. I asked him some questions about how a stroke had been ruled out and how the ear infection diagnosis had been settled on. He was irritated and rattled off some medical jargon in a condescending tone. His pompous attitude angered me and I began to fire questions at him.

He retorted back more medical "yada yada yada". Our verbal battle ended with his threat to discharge her immediately.

He turned from me and stomped over to Nissa's bed. There was still a hint of irritation in his voice as he started shooting questions at her. When she did not respond, he raised his voice to the kind of shouting cadence one uses with someone who is hard of hearing.

When he couldn't rouse her enough to complete a respectable medical exam, he announced that she could stay until the afternoon but she would be going home that day. I hoped that his indignant march out of the room was justified and that I was being the irritating, ill-informed family member that he saw me as.

Nissa's husband had also stayed in the hospital room, napping on and off during the night. He was happy to let me take on the doctor with all of the unanswered questions. I suggested that he go home and check on the kids or get some sleep or do whatever he had planned on doing that day and I would stay with Nissa.

Our mother lives about five hours south of us. She packed up right away and was at Nissa's side by afternoon. That evening it appeared as if Nissa had totally recovered. She was walking, talking, eating, voiding, and whatever else that would indicate she was medically stable.

A different doctor did evening rounds. Nissa told him she didn't feel right and really didn't want to go home yet. For some reason, he agreed to keep her one more night. I went home thinking that maybe my gut instincts had been wrong. I still suspected that we didn't know what had happened, but was also tired and wanted to get some sleep.

I was awakened early the next morning by the phone ringing. I don't remember who called but the news was disturbing. Nissa had rung the nurse's station sometime after midnight and asked for some pain medication. She told the nurse she had a bad headache. She was discovered several hours later slumped over, drooling, and unable to respond.

A neurologist had been summoned and a CAT scan completed, but nothing was found. The neurologist suggested that Nissa was having psychological problems and was catatonic (a psychiatric condition where one is unable to move, appearing frozen). Upon hearing that, Nissa's husband decided to have her transferred to a larger hospital with a different medical team.

Teena and I got dressed and headed to the larger hospital in Salt Lake City, about an hour away. A doctor with an exotic sounding name met us immediately after Nissa's arrival by ambulance. He had heard the other medical team's theories.

I was greatly relieved and impressed when his first question was, "What do you think has happened?" He allowed us to tell him our thoughts and feelings and listened carefully and respectfully to our strong disagreement with the "psychotic" theory. He was certain that an MRI would help with the unanswered questions.

It took hours to do the MRI. Nissa's body was wreathing with involuntary movements and she had to be sedated at deeper and deeper levels to accomplish the stillness necessary to capture images of her brain.

The doctor's dark, east-Indian complexion looked pale as he approached us with the verdict. He took a deep, labored breath before making eye contact with us. His compassionate nature radiated through his eyes. I was moved that he was willing to feel the emotion behind the message he was about to deliver. His voice was apologetic but deliberate.

"It's not good," he started steadily. "There is a large blood clot lodged in her mid brain. There is evidence of another neurological event in the right vertebral artery at the base of her brain."

He wasn't sure what to make of it but said he needed to start a very dangerous medical procedure immediately.

"Coumiden is a blood-thinning agent that may help dissolve the blood clot; but it may also cause her brain to bleed, resulting in her death. I need your permission to proceed."

A heavy silence descended as questions started drifting in my mind: What if we proceed and it kills her? What if we don't proceed and she dies from the lack of treatment? The doctor waited patiently as we searched each other's faces for answers.

"May I proceed?" he gently asked.

Her husband reluctantly gave permission. I nodded in agreement, and in support of him. Taking some action seemed like a better risk than inaction. I had confidence in this doctor and he seemed to think it was a good risk to take.

The next time I saw Nissa, she was in the intensive care unit (ICU). Her neck had been neatly sliced and a tracheotomy tube placed in the incision. Her chest heaved as it was blown full of air by a ventilator.

I felt a sense of violation as I observed how the machines penetrated and controlled her body. I came to hate the hissing sound that accompanied the release of air as her body sunk helplessly into the hospital bed only to be forced full of air again and again.

Tears began to stream down my cheeks as I looked at her limp body being kept alive by the hideous machines. I left the room until I could compose myself.

The reality of her possible death hit me hard as I stood outside her room. It really looked like she was already gone. I tried to control my voice enough to call home. I asked my husband, Tim, to bring Mom up to the hospital and warned that it may be the last time we all see Nissa alive. I chose not be there when our mother went in to see her. I didn't want to witness her emotion. I had enough of my own to deal with.

I don't remember where I went but I left for a while. When I returned I saw three men in white shirts, ties, and suit coats file out of Nissa's room. I studied their unfamiliar faces. The first one looked like he had seen a ghost. I wondered if the sight of her on a ventilator had affected him like it had me. I was surprised to see the other two looking much the same way. I naturally wondered what was going on.

My brother, Shane, was at the end of the procession leaving the room. I got up and walked toward him. When the three had passed safely by I asked, "What is going on? What happened in there?"

"They gave her a blessing," he reported in a confident voice. I assumed from his comment that they were men from her congregation that had come to pray for her.

"Why do they all look like someone just slapped 'em?" My sarcasm was inappropriate, but provided an adequate diversion from the intense emotion surrounding the whole situation.

"He just called down the powers of Heaven to heal her. It was a very moving blessing. The feelings in the room were powerful." Shane's voice was distant. He was obviously still processing the experience.

We were called together as a family later that evening. The attending physician wanted to talk to us. He had been assigned the case and elected to come in on Sunday night to have this discussion. It was evident from his dress pants and button down shirt that he was not working this shift and had made a special trip in for the occasion.

He kept his message simple, his voice monotone, and his eyes mostly looking at the ground. There was a hint of irritation or some kind of protective edge carefully guarding his emotion so that none could be detected. I couldn't tell if it was his version of being professional, if he was struggling with his own emotion, or just irritated to be called in on a day off.

"The way you see her today is the way she will remain until you decide to let her go. She is being kept alive artificially by machines. She has a zero percent chance of recovery. It is recommended that you call the family together and say goodbye to her and then release her. There is no purpose in keeping her like this. It would be very expensive for your family to keep her on life support."

It took a while for the sterile words to sink in. It wasn't what we expected to hear. My sister-in-law, Linda, finally volleyed him a challenge.

"Zero percent chance of recovery? You mean there is no chance at all that she can recover?"

The doctor conceded his exaggeration and said, "OK, she may have a five percent chance of recovery but it is highly unlikely that she will ever gain any functionality. She will be much like you see her today."

Linda was not going to give up that easy. "If this was your wife and you had a one-month-old baby, would you just pull the plug and let her go?"

All eyes were now on the doctor who looked to be in his late 30's and could possibly relate to this being his wife. He shuffled nervously as his guarded, physician self wrestled with his personal feelings. I'm not sure why he abandoned his physician façade to be personal, but his defenses dropped for a minute.

"If it were my wife," he paused long enough that we all intensified our collective gaze at him. "I would keep her on life support and fight for stem cell research."

His confession was a little surprising to me. He told us what he was supposed to tell us which was that we should let her go, but also had the courage to admit that it was not what he would do.

"We are close to having the technology to restore people like this, but there is a huge political battle still ahead. Stem cell research is her only hope".

He paused politely while we attempted to absorb that piece of information and then he continued. "You should decide within a couple days. When you've made a decision, we can help you with how to proceed."

He gave another obligatory pause and then asked, "Do you have any other questions?" The tone of his voice clearly indicated that he was done with the conversation.

We honored his unspoken request to be dismissed by answering "No".

It had been a very long day and I decided not to think or feel any more. I don't remember driving home from Salt Lake City, nor do I remember if I got any sleep that night. I do remember returning the next day and standing for hours over her seemingly lifeless body while an internal battle raged inside of me.

I know enough about neurology to know that once brain cells die their function is lost. Brain cells do not regenerate like other cells in the body. I know that when adult brains sustain injuries, they typically are unable to completely heal or recover previous functioning. Brain damage is irreversible. At least, that is what I had been taught, and certainly what I had seen thus far in life.

On the other hand, I believe that spiritual powers govern and supersede this life's perceived physical realities. That is why I believe in miracles. My spiritual side argued that it was a matter of faith. To me, faith is the act of consciously calling forth the energy of intention to bring about change in the physical realm. My doubting thoughts were evidence of my lack of faith or confused intentions. Faith would need to be exercised before a miracle would be possible. I wondered if her healing would be brought about by the faith of those who surrounded her, or hindered by those who believed it was impossible.

My logical mind argued that it was naïve to believe she could ever really heal. She was completely paralyzed and unconscious. The doctors said there was substantial brain damage. My problem was that I had worked with many people who struggled with brain injuries and I knew the reality. I had seen it over and over again. I really knew that she would never be the same, so what miracle could I hope for, pray for, and really believe?

I desperately wanted to see something to believe in, but struggled to know what that was. If there were some sign of life in her it would be easier to believe she could be healed. However, she was being kept alive by machines, and so my internal battle between fact and faith raged on.

At the moment, a big decision needed to be made. Would we take her off life support, or artificially prolong her life with the expensive machines?

I felt at peace about that question. I would vote that the machines be turned off and believed that she would breathe on her own. This, however, was not because of my faith. She had breathed for about 12 hours on her own before she was hooked up to life support. It made sense to me that she would breathe on her own if the machines

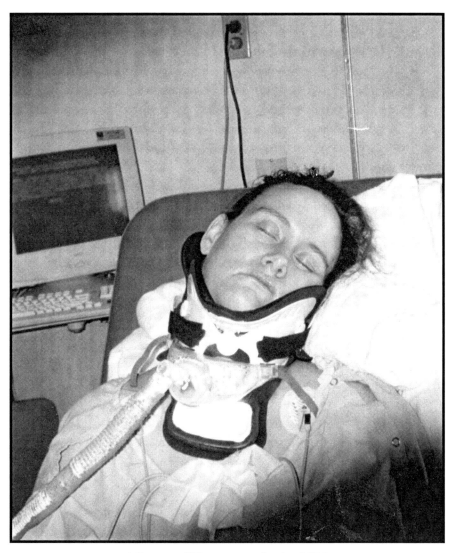

Nissa on life support in the ICU

were disconnected. I didn't think her respiratory function had been disabled by the stroke. My bigger question revolved around what would happen after that.

Before I left that night, I felt compelled to speak out loud to her. "Nissa," I called softly as if she could hear me.

"I don't understand what has happened to you. I don't know why God would send your beautiful baby here if he intended to call you home. You are in a really big mess and I don't know how you're going to get out of it if you decide to stay. If you choose to go, I'll help take care of your girls. I'll tell them about you. I'll do what I can for them."

I paused while redirecting my thoughts and then went on. "But if you decide to stay, I'll walk with you every step of the way."

I kissed her softly on the forehead and then cried all the way to the parking lot. It felt like I had just told her goodbye, but I wasn't sure. I had surrendered to whatever was going to happen and quit trying to guess what that might be. I was ready to turn off the machines and accept whatever followed.

CHAPTER 2

The Next Step

"I'll walk with you every step of the way." The words came from somewhere inside of me, escaping my lips in a whispered tone. In the moments that followed, my body filled with an awareness that felt heavy. I had a vague notion that I was about to embark on a difficult journey. My conscious mind struggled to grasp what a deeper part of me seemed to already know, but nothing really came into focus. All I really knew was that Nissa was in God's hands and I had some role to play in this unfolding story.

The following morning, the doctor with the exotic sounding name arrived at Nissa's side shortly after I did. He radiated hope as he started his simple neurological exam. Nissa's eyes were open but starred into space and had no signs of recognition or responsiveness in them. The rest of her body remained totally still. There was no evidence that she could feel or move any part of her body.

His dark eyes revealed a sense of confidence as he looked up and pronounced, "We are going to take this one day at a time. You never know."

I wondered what he was thinking but he left before I transitioned from wondering to asking. He certainly had a different perspective than the "pull the plug" doctor from the previous evening. I was confused that a neurologist would have a sense of hope in this situation. I wondered what he knew that I didn't know.

The Monday morning staff at the hospital brought a whole new atmosphere to the ICU. Her body was being moved in, what seemed like, anticipation that she would recover some of her ability to function. I wasn't sure why 12 hours and a new crew of caretakers would create such a change.

The left side of Nissa's neck was in a constant spasm, curling the left side of her head into her left shoulder. She had been strapped into a neck brace in an attempt to keep her head positioned between her shoulders, instead of drawn to the side. The neck brace helped some, but her head still pulled to the left. Tennis shoes had been wrestled onto her feet because the muscles in her left foot were contracting causing her toes to curl under.

One of the ICU nurses joined family members as we gathered around the bed to discuss the plan for the day. The nurse expressed her opinion that Nissa was more aware than we knew. We asked why she thought that. She said that she used to work on a rehab unit and had seen other people in similar conditions.

"Do you mind if we do an experiment?" she asked.

We looked at each other, shrugged our shoulders, and said, "Go ahead."

She then stood over Nissa so that her eyes were directly over Nissa's open eyes and said, "If you can hear my voice, blink your eyes."

We all leaned in toward Nissa and stared at her eyes. Three or four seconds went by as her eyes slowly closed. We then looked up and surveyed each other's eyes to determine what we all thought. It was unanimous. We were all confused about whether she intentionally closed her eyes, or if they just closed on their own.

The nurse was not deterred. "Nissa, if you can hear my voice, blink your eyes twice."

Clever, I thought, as I intently watched while the next ten seconds went by. Nissa managed to close her eyes twice, but really slowly. This time we all looked at each other with excitement in our eyes.

"Nissa, you can hear us?" I asked, still not sure if I could believe it. Sure enough, her eyes slowly closed again.

"Nissa, I'm going to ask you some questions. I want you to blink once for 'yes' and twice for 'no'. Is that OK with you?" the nurse asked kindly.

The nurse established a connection with Nissa and clearly demonstrated that she was right. Nissa was definitely there and very much aware. The family members, who watched this simple miracle, were infused with new hope.

This nurse believed the doctors were wrong and acted on her belief. She believed, for whatever reason, that she could reach Nissa, which she did. Her beliefs and actions opened a big door that day.

We quickly adapted to the world of "yes" and "no" questions. The more Nissa blinked out the answers the more control she gained over the muscles in her eyes. Her blinking response was still very slow, but her ability to communicate created a whole new dimension to the situation-especially the part about pulling the plug and letting her go.

Communication efforts got more sophisticated as the day went on. We found a way for Nissa to communicate back. We would start reciting the alphabet, very slowly, one letter at a time. When we arrived at the appropriate letter, Nissa would blink. We would then start over at the first of the alphabet in search of the next letter and continue the routine until we arrived at a word.

If we recited the letters too quickly, we would go by the appropriate letter before she was able to blink so finding the proper rhythm was crucial. We sometimes had to guess what the word was because the letters we thought she had blinked at didn't spell anything. It was a tedious process.

We eventually learned some shortcuts. We started guessing early in the game so we could avoid the painfully slow recitations. We also started grouping the letters in rows with four or five letters to a row. We wrote the letters out on a paper or dry erase board, held it over her face, and then asked if the letter she wanted was on the first row, second row, etc. She would blink at the appropriate row. Then we would start down the row, naming the individual letters until we got a blink.

It sometimes took several minutes to get from one letter to the next. By the time we got to the next letter, we often had forgotten the preceding letter or letters. We eventually developed a system where we had one alphabet board and one transcription board so we could record each letter as we went along and see our progress. If early on it didn't add up to a word, we could back track more easily.

Nissa learned to talk in short hand. She would spell bits and pieces of what she wanted to say and we would guess the rest using her affirmative blink if we were on the right track and no blink if we were off track. That day, it became unmistakably clear that Nissa was very much present in a body that she had no command of whatsoever except, of course, for her eyes.

The big question of whether to pull the plug became even more complicated that day. It was obvious to me that it was no longer a family or medical decision. Nissa was fully here and would need to make her own decision about her life.

Would she choose to live like this? Was there a chance that she could recover after all? Would she have the courage to stay or the courage to say goodbye? Neither looked like pretty options from my perspective.

I wondered what her doctor would tell her. I wondered what he thought about the discovery that Nissa's mind was fully functioning. I wondered what I should say to her. I wondered if this was a gift-one last chance to connect with her before she died. The whole situation was still very unclear.

Nissa had some questions of her own. "How long has it been?" was one of the first things she asked. She was aware that she had been disconnected from her life, and in and out of consciousness, but didn't have any way to gage the amount of time she had lost.

"What will happen to the girls?" We couldn't tell if she was thinking she was going to die, or if she was just worried about being able to take care of the children. At this stage, we hadn't said anything to her about her medical prognosis. We reassured her that the girls were fine and had many people who loved them to help take care of them.

Her question however raised another big issue: What should we tell the children?

12-10-01 5:00 PM	WHAT WILL HAPPEN TO THE GIRLS
12-11-01 11:00 AM	TAKE OFF SHOES
12-11-01 2:30 PM	TAKE THE ~~MOENS~~ SHOE
TO SHYLEE & MCKENZIE 12-11-01 4:35 PM	I LOVE YOU
12-11-01 5:00 PM	MY NECK HURTS

Page from a notebook where communication
was transcribed one eye blink at a time.

CHAPTER 3

The Children

Should they see her like this? What if they never see her again? Should this be the last picture in their mind of their mother? Shylee was six years old and McKenzie was three. They were used to seeing their mother every day. How long could they or should they be kept from what was happening? Would it traumatize them to see their mother hooked up to all the machines, unable to talk or touch them?

I wondered what effect the children would have on Nissa if they came to see her. Would she want the children to see her like this? Would she want to see them one last time if she knew she was going to die? Would seeing them help her to hold on, fight back, or move forward?

I don't remember who made the decision or how it was made but I remember driving to the hospital with the girls. Their father drove and I talked.

"Mommy can't talk or move her body. She is in a hospital bed and won't be able to look at you or say 'hi' or pick you up. All she can do right now is blink her eyes. Mommy has machines helping her breath so there is a tube in her throat." I tried to prepare them the best I could for what they were about to experience.

ICU's have an atmosphere that is naturally tense. Children

are not usually allowed in them for a variety of reasons. The staff allowed these little ones in because they knew it may be the last time they ever saw their mother - or their mother them. I think the staff also knew that it might have a positive impact on Nissa to see her children.

The meeting was more intense than I had anticipated. The other function that Nissa had gained was the ability to cry. However, once she started to cry she did not have the ability to stop. The tracheotomy prevented any sound from being produced when she cried, but her face would contort into a very unnatural, tortured looking spasm that was disturbing to see and would continue for long periods of time.

It started as soon as we lifted the girls up and held them over her face so she could see them. We immediately set the girls back down so they couldn't see her, or at least not see her face. It was disturbing for adults to see the facial contortions and unbridled pain that poured from her eyes. It didn't seem like a wise thing to expose the children to.

I went back to the waiting area with the girls. Kenzie quickly sighted the toys and went to work playing with the new discoveries. Shylee was unusually quiet and withdrawn. She wouldn't verbalize anything about what was going on inside of her and just shook her head "no" to any questions that we asked.

When Nissa finally quit crying, we decided to give it another try. Kenzie was eager to see Mom again. It was all a big adventure to her. She didn't seem to see the machines or mind that Mommy couldn't talk. Kenzie was happy to just be by her mother's side and touch her.

Shylee was more deeply impacted by the whole situation. She did not want to go back in the room.

Something about what she experienced was too much. She had retreated to a deeper place inside and wanted to stay there for now. She didn't want to play, didn't want to talk, and didn't want to see Mommy again. I wondered if it had been a mistake to bring them.

It took several exposures to the children before Nissa could see them and not cry. Shylee eventually came in again and watched

McKenzie (3) and Shylee (6)

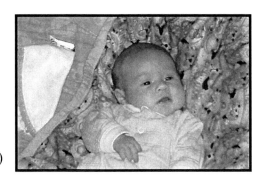

Carli (1 month)

while we did some eye blink communications. She seemed to grasp that her mother was still in there somewhere.

Then there was Carli J. She had been with her mother 24 hours a day for the first month of her life. Now her mother was gone. Nissa couldn't hold her, nurse her, talk to her, or connect with her in any way. What impact would the sudden disconnect have on her? Was there anything we could do to lessen the impact? These were questions that went unanswered while Carli's paternal grandmother scooped her up and did all she could to be a maternal surrogate.

Visits to the ICU with the children on the days that followed were lighter and more playful. We made a game of counting as the elevator ascended to the appropriate floor. It was almost like a game of hide and seek to discover which room Mom was in that day. The children quickly acclimated to the new event in their lives.

CHAPTER 4

Aunt Bubbles

The girls started living with their grandmother on their father's side of the family, Grandma Lou. She was headed to the hospital one evening with the girls and I was along for the trip for some reason. Nissa was still in the ICU.

The girls were at ease now seeing their "sick" Mom who had tubes coming and going from her immobile body. They seemed to understand that she couldn't talk and amused themselves with the novelty of the hospital environment.

It was dark when we left the hospital to head home. There aren't many gas stations in downtown Salt Lake City, but we needed to find one before getting onto the freeway to go home. It was winter and very cold. I was tired and stressed. I'm sure the girls could feel my tension. They were overly animated and silly.

We found a gas station and Grandma Lou got out of the car to fill it up. I was in the front seat on the passenger side of the car in my nice, black leather jacket. I laid my head back against the headrest on my seat and closed my eyes. My mind shut down and my emotions numbed. I needed a rest.

I had tuned out the children's chatter in the back seat until it erupted into laughter, then louder laughter. I slowly opened my eyes and turned enough to see into the back seat. As my tired adult eyes met their innocent gleeful eyes, the laughter stopped, but only for a second or two.

Their little fingers pointed my way and then they burst out laughing again.

"What's so funny?" I demanded in a teasing voice.

"Bubbles", they said through their laughter.

"What?" I asked, not understanding what was going on.

One of them leaned forward, pointed toward my shoulder, and managed to get the word "bubbles" out between her spurts of laughter.

I looked down at my shoulder and sure enough it was covered with bubbles. The puzzled look on my face evoked another attack of giggles from the girls.

Someone had bought them little pocket sized bubble blowers at the hospital gift shop. These, however, were not ordinary soap bubbles. They were some sort of super, duper, plasticky, not-easily-popped sort of bubbles.

I was wearing a leather jacket that was now covered with plastic bubbles, as was my head and my lap. The girls sent bubbles flying from the back seat of the car and they all seemed to gravitate right to me and my nice leather jacket.

Then the girls started trying to pop the bubbles that were all over me. I noticed that when they popped, they left a thin, round blob of plasticky stuff behind. My leather jacket was slowly being covered with blobs of plastic that I could not brush off. I hollered for them to stop, which, of course just made them laugh and blow bubbles all the faster.

I quickly realized that there wasn't much I could do but surrender. If my jacket was ruined, a few more spots weren't going to hurt, and if it was redeemable, they may as well enjoy pelting me with as many bubbles as possible.

I decided to join the fun and pulled faces and acted silly while they continued to laugh at the bubbles collecting on my head.

"Look, its bubble head," one of them said.

"Aunt Bubbles," the other one replied.

I didn't know the name would stick even longer than the bubbles, but that is exactly what happened. For the next two years I was affectionately referred to as "Aunt Bubbles" whenever the girls were around.

Shortly after that, they decided my husband also needed a new name and dubbed him "Uncle Lumpy". Aunt Bubbles and Uncle Lumpy slowly took on new roles in the lives of the girls and were woven into the emotional fabric that would wrap them with another layer of loving support.

CHAPTER 5

Believe

At some time during the first few days in the ICU, the doctors decided to decrease the respiratory support to see what would happen. Nissa's respiratory muscles functioned voluntarily but were not strong enough to produce adequate oxygen to sustain her. It was however evident that she could survive without life support so the respirator was replaced with an oxygen tube.

This experiment evidently eliminated the necessity of making the "big decision." I never saw the "pull the plug, she has zero chance of recovery" doctor again, so I am not sure who was calling the medical shots after the first day.

The doctor with the exotic sounding name came by each morning and performed his simple neurological exam. Each day when there was no progress he still looked up and confidently announced, "one day at a time."

I loved it when he came in even though I didn't understand what he was thinking. He radiated compassion and kept a small flame of hope kindled. He was quiet with his words, allowing the family members facing him to hear while the professional world around him only saw the simple exam. He slipped in and out of the room so quickly each morning that I never had a chance to question him.

The next event I remember was the announcement that Nissa would be discharged to a nursing home. The news was shocking. How could she go from the most intense medical unit the hospital offers to the minimal medical care that a nursing home provides? Since pulling the plug was no longer a consideration, maybe they thought it best to let her die on her own with no medical care.

We were told she would spend one or two days in a regular hospital bed and then be discharged to the nursing home of our choosing. Even that sounded like too big of a transition too fast. There were so many unanswered medical questions. I got the distinct feeling that she was being prematurely flushed from the medical system to a human repository for broken bodies.

The frantic search for a nursing home began. We got a list of nursing homes from the hospital social worker and divided the task of visiting them. After the first few visits we got back together to compare notes. It was grim at best.

The one that smelt like a urinal had a loving, caring staff but I had to hold my breath and concentrate on not throwing up as I walked through the halls. Another one had better air quality but the staff scared me with their less-than-professional presentation. There was one that didn't smell too bad and the staff appeared attentive, however the residents were in such sad shape that I feared it would send a powerfully negative message to Nissa about her own condition.

We finally found a nursing home that seemed benign. It didn't smell bad, the halls were not lined with broken bodies, the staff looked professional, there was an empty private room with a window, and it was close to a hospital. The room was at the end of a hallway where it would be private. It had wallpaper with pink roses just like Nissa liked and was close to respiratory equipment if there was some emergency need for it.

Back at the hospital things were very intense. Nissa cried nearly all of the time. The spasms in her body were constant and the staff caring for her was clueless about what to do to help her. The step down from intensive to regular care was dramatic. It became apparent that family members needed to be there to coach the hospital staff about Nissa's care.

I entered her room one afternoon with the intention of talking to her about our search for a placement. Her neck was curled dramatically to the side and she was in tears. I asked the nurse in the room if he had tried to communicate with her. He mentioned that he had asked her if she needed anything but she didn't talk to him so he figured she was OK. I asked him if he knew she was paralyzed. He answered "yes." I was stunned. I then asked him if he knew that she couldn't talk. This time he was stunned and said "no."

A few hours later a new nurse was on shift. Nissa's neck again was knotted into her shoulder and she was crying. I asked the new nurse if she had tried to help Nissa. She said she had straightened out Nissa's neck but Nissa immediately moved it back so she figured that was how Nissa wanted her neck. I nearly cried this time.

It scared me to see how quickly she was misunderstood and left alone. The staff didn't have the time or interest to understand her and quickly did what little they thought they needed to do and then left. I didn't know at the time, but this was only a preview of what was to come.

We told Nissa about the nursing home that had been selected. All she could do was cry. I think she must have been scared but I'm not sure.

A New-Age type massage therapist came to visit on Nissa's last night in the hospital. The massage therapist knew Nissa from before the stroke, and we thought she might be able to help. She said Nissa was attempting to let go of something and if she were successful at letting it go that her body would return to normal. It sounded like a long shot to me, but her presence seemed to give Nissa a flicker of hope and comfort.

Nissa cried the whole time the massage therapist was there, but through the tears there was some kind of reaching out to connect. Nissa seemed to respond to the touch and the emotional connection.

Teena found little, blue picture frames in the gift shop that had the word "Believe" written across the bottom of them. She bought every one they had and mounted a beautiful picture of Nissa in each one. She then distributed the pictures to family members.

"Believe" became the motto that united us. Believing was the lifeline that we wrapped around Nissa and held on to as we moved to the next level of the journey.

"Believe" became our theme.

CHAPTER 6

Nursing Home Blues

In the ICU there were monitors 24 hours a day on all of Nissa's vital signs. There were nurses a few steps away that observed her several times each hour. There was always someone available and knowledgeable to answer questions. The ICU is one of the most intense levels of medical care available.

The nursing home was a huge contrast. The doctor did rounds once a month, except during the holidays when he was taking time off. The staff refused to page him to answer questions or make medication adjustments. He was only to be paged if it was a life-or-death situation. His most frequent page was probably to tell him that one of the nursing home residents had died.

There were different nurses on shift each day and most weekends. Most of the nurses had full-time jobs elsewhere and took random shifts at the nursing home to make extra money. They were usually too busy to answer questions. Most of the care was provided by Certified Nurse's Assistants (CNAs) who had little experience and only minimal medical training.

It didn't take long for me to figure out that the younger woman (staff often commented on how young she was to be in a nursing home), who couldn't talk, in the room at the end of the hall far away from the nurse's station, would receive only minimal care and no monitoring. It's not that the staff didn't care or were negligent. It was more that the squeaky wheels get the grease and Nissa was not able to squeak.

Nissa was on an arsenal of medication. It was difficult to determine if any of it was doing any good. The doctor was unavailable for consultation and did not actively take over her care. He merely continued the medication regime that was started in the ICU.

Medically, we felt totally abandoned and alone. The prognosis was "she'll be like this until she dies." I got the impression that most expected her to die sooner rather than later. The nursing home was a place to keep her comfortable until she passed away. There was no point in doing much other than seeing to her comfort but no one seemed to know what to do to make her comfortable. So she was mostly just left alone.

There were some attempts at therapy. A physical therapist came in a couple of times a week to do range of motion exercises and roll her around a little. The point was not to rehabilitate but to keep her from total deterioration physically. We learned about bedsores, immobile muscles, and other topics related to long-term paralysis. Family members were trained and encouraged to do systematic muscle manipulation whenever they visited. Movement was important to circulation, which was important to tissue health.

A speech therapist named Tim came several times a week to work on communication options and skills. Tim worked full time at the hospital across the street but came to the nursing home to see a few patients. He brought picture boards that had daily living activities on them.

The idea was that staff could point at pictures and Nissa could blink "yes" or "no" if she was interested in that activity. The problem was that Nissa was not capable of many of those activities. Tim continued to come and continued pursue options. He seemed to have a genuine interest in helping Nissa in some way.

From my perspective, the cavalry was not coming. Traditional medicine had reached its peak and had little to offer other than minor comfort. I started to look at the world of alternative medicine.

I had a physician acquaintance that, in the prime of his life, had an abscessed tooth that created a heart attack that lead to a stroke. I knew he had reached beyond his traditional medical background to alternative sources in his own recovery. I called him to see if he would give me some direction. He freely shared his experience and made suggestions.

I continued exploring and came across unusual stories of recovery from various medical maladies. I studied the whys and wherefores of remedies and gadgets. In the end, I decided to try what the physician friend had said he thought had helped him.

I repeated what I thought I had learned to Nissa and asked for her input. After all, she was the one that had to live with the results - or lack thereof. Together we decided where to start and how fast to go.

Essential oils were a part of my world before all of this happened to Nissa. I had brought oils in that were known to cross the blood/brain barrier and started administering them when she was in the ICU. I had hoped the oils would move some oxygen or some kind of nourishment to the part of her brain that had been damaged. We continued experimenting with oils in the nursing home.

Our biggest adventure was a contraption called "The Rattler." The inventor was a fellow who suffered severe injuries to his legs and was told that they would need to be amputated. He pled with his doctors to give him a chance to rehabilitate. He was an inventor and came up with a machine that sent electrical signals through the body at frequencies compatible with the body's own energy. The result - he was able to rehabilitate his legs and now walks as normal as ever.

I purchased a Rattler from him and was trained on its use. I would sneak it into the nursing home in a large satchel and get it out when I knew there would not be interruptions. The Rattler had two paddles that were about eight inches long, three inches wide, and made of a piece of flat rubber. The paddles housed an electrical devise that sent out the current of energy. The inventor instructed me to put one paddle on the right side of her head (the side that controls the left side of the body) and one paddle on her left hand or foot (the side that was paralyzed). He suggested I keep it on as long as she could tolerate it.

Once I got her hooked up and flipped the switch, I would gradually increase the intensity until she blinked that it was enough. At first she could only tolerate a few minutes. Eventually, she built up to about 15 minutes at a time.

There was one big problem. When I flipped the switch, it knocked out the television reception in all of the nearby rooms. If we happened to have a mobile neighbor, they would complain to the staff, who would then come see what the problem was. If staff ever came down the hall, I shut the machine off so they wouldn't come in the room. The machine made a loud, scary noise that sounded like a giant rattlesnake. I suppose that is how it got its name. I did get busted once by a nurse. She was very unhappy about the Rattler being used in the nursing home and very suspicious of me for bringing it in. She threatened to have me banned from the nursing home. I don't remember what I said to her, but I did get her calmed down enough that I didn't get kicked out.

I didn't really know if any of this would help. I did have a strong feeling that if Nissa was meant to live, it shouldn't be like this. If she was meant to die, so be it. I was more interested in looking for solutions than sitting day after day waiting for something to happen. I chose to believe there was hope and acted on that belief in whatever way I could.

I also started to realize at a deeper level that I could believe what I see or see what I believe. And that consciously making a choice between the two was crucial.

CHAPTER 7

The Minister

Nights became especially difficult for Nissa. Staff would come around at about 10:00 p.m. and turn the lights out. She would often lay in the same position all night, all alone, in the dark, in pain, and be unable to sleep. She was also unable to call the staff to let them know she needed something.

She would prefer to have the TV going all night than to be alone in the dark, but nobody ever asked. She would prefer to have a regular dose of medication for the pain, but it did not come regularly. She would prefer to be moved once or twice a night, but if she didn't ask she didn't receive - she had no way to ask. It seemed like educating her caretakers was a continual process.

My life became consumed with helping to care for her. I had a business that I worked from 8 to 5. I would then go to the nursing home three or four nights a week and stay until Nissa had received her evening dose of medication. I made it a point to talk to the night staff before I left to make sure they knew that she was in the room at the end of the hall and would need to be checked on and receive additional medication during the night.

On this particular night something was different. I could see in her eyes that something was wrong. I started guessing but couldn't quite figure it out so we started the spelling routine.

It turned out that she wanted a blessing. She needed something to hang on to that I couldn't give her and that wouldn't come from the nursing home staff. She needed the kind of comfort that comes from a spiritual source.

It was nearly 10:00 p.m. The time I usually left for home. Nissa was from a community 30 minutes to the north, so everyone she knew was at least a half hour away. I was from a town 30 minutes to the south so everyone I knew was also at least a half hour away. Most people would be in bed at this hour. I wasn't sure who to call or what to tell them about why we needed them.

I asked her if she could wait until tomorrow. She blinked "no." She wanted the blessing tonight. I had to fight back my own tears. I was exhausted and wanted to go home myself. I honestly didn't know whom to call. I began to pray and hoped that she would just fall asleep, giving me until tomorrow to fulfill her request.

The room next door was occupied by someone who required a respiratory therapist to be there at all times. The same therapist came in most evenings and was in the room next door while I was with Nissa. I had to pass that room to get to Nissa's so would often see him but had never spoken to him.

On this particular evening, I had noticed that he kept pacing to the end of the hall and then would glance into Nissa's room before he turned to walk back. It was unusual for him to pace like this and he seemed uneasy about something.

I had been praying for about 15 minutes when he stepped hesitantly into the room. He projected a timid demeanor, knowing that he had just walked uninvited into our space. I looked up and smiled to let him know that it was okay that he was there. I was very curious about why he had come in.

"Do you mind if I come in?" His voice was soft, but more confident than his body language had been.

"Please do." I motioned for him to join me by Nissa's side.

He then walked over and looked down into Nissa's eyes and smiled. He introduced himself as the respiratory therapist for the patient next door. Nissa, of course, just starred at him since that is all she could do. I nodded my head affirmatively and smiled again.

He made some kind of small talk for a minute or two. I was beginning to wonder if he was just bored and wanted to pass the time by visiting. If that was the case, I thought maybe it would distract Nissa from her concerns; or maybe he would keep her company while I went home. But maybe he was one of those weirdoes that do bad things to vulnerable people so maybe I wouldn't be able to leave at all.

I think he saw me drifting off so he shifted away from the small talk.

"I'm also a minister." His words were laced with courage.

My eyes widened. He definitely had my attention. "Really, where is your congregation?" I was truly curious.

"I have a small congregation in Salt Lake." He seemed proud.

"What religion?" I asked.

I don't remember how he answered that question but I do remember that he quickly moved into his agenda for coming into the room. In the small-talk portion of our meeting he had learned that Nissa was paralyzed and that I was her sister. He had also asked what religion we were.

"Would it offend you if someone not of your faith prayed for her?" His question was sincere.

I could hardly believe my ears. I looked down into Nissa's eyes and asked her, "Would you like the minister to pray for you?"

She blinked once for "yes."

I explained the blink system of communication to him so he would understand how to read her and then translated that she had just said "yes".

He stepped closer to her and asked, "Would she mind if I took her hand?"

I smiled down at her and repeated the question, "Do you mind if he takes your hand?"

Her eyes smiled back as she delivered the double blink answer of "no."

I looked up at him and nodded my head affirmatively as I said, "It's OK if you take her hand."

With that permission he shifted into an official posture. He took her spasming left hand and placed it confidently between his strong masculine hands. He then looked compassionately into her eyes and paused for a moment before beginning a very powerful prayer.

He told her that God loved her and was mindful of her. He said that this situation was no accident and that God saw this day before she was even born. This whole experience was part of a plan and somehow was for her good. He repeated several times that God loved her and was with her.

She began to cry as soon as he began to talk. I cried too. I was touched that God answered her prayer that night. She needed him and he found a way to connect to her. God found a way around my limitations and sent his servant to help us both.

When the minister finished the prayer, he continued to hold her hand until she and I both were able to quit crying. He was very kind and seemed relieved to have been able to complete his little mission that night.

It was suddenly clear to me that his pacing earlier was because he was being prompted to come to us, but it took a while to work up the nerve. After all, he was there as a professional charged with the care of the patient next door and not as a minister to the woman at the end of the hall.

I thanked God all the way home for sending the minister to us. I admired his courage and appreciated the confident way he carried out his charge. I wondered how it would affect Nissa. I hoped it was what she needed.

The next day I questioned Nissa about the previous night. She indicated that she slept well and had a good night. The effect lasted for weeks. She didn't seem to dread the 10 o'clock lights-out routine as much. She seemed more confident and at peace.

The minister had a lasting effect on me as well. I felt sometimes like we were wandering through a medical wilderness with no compass or manna. The minister reminded me that if I let God lead it would be less of a burden to me. I didn't need to figure it out; I just needed to listen to the voice of inspiration and have the courage to act on it. Something in me healed that night too. I was no longer afraid of the darkness we were in.

CHAPTER 8

The Butterfly and the Bell

"Locked in Syndrome" emerged as the medical slang to describe her condition. It was kind of like how Lou Gehrig's disease eventually leaves its victims - a mind in tact locked in a body that is totally immobile.

The nursing home doctor did rounds at unpredictable times and was taking time off for the holidays so he was not available for information. The doctors from the hospital ICU were now a part of the past. We wanted to know the prognosis for someone who was "locked in" but had no one to turn to for an answer, so we began to do our own research on the topic.

Professional literature was hard to come by and what we did find didn't tell us much. I contacted doctors that I knew here or there and asked them about "locked in syndrome." Many didn't have any idea what I was talking about. The fact that this was rare and unknown to the medical community was slowly coming into focus and "locked in syndrome" seemed to be more of a description than a disorder or diagnosis.

We then turned to non-professional literature and found a story about a girl in her twenties, Judy Mozersky, who had something similar happen. She too had a stroke that was misdiagnosed initially and resulted in paralysis. She was able to recover to the extent that she was paraplegic. She was able to live semi-independently. There was a picture of her in a motorized wheelchair on the cover of the book. She drove the wheelchair with a control knob that her non-paralyzed hand was able to manipulate.

The story of her defiant recovery was both hopeful and disappointing. I would rather have read that she completely recovered, but it was clearly miraculous that she had gotten as far as she had. The book had a positive theme and a feel-good message. I tried to sell the story to Nissa as a hopeful sign that she too could recover, but I think it left both of us feeling sad. It's not how we wanted the story to end.

The next book we found was called "The Diving Bell and the Butterfly." It was written by a professional writer who, in his late forties, had a stroke that left him totally paralyzed except for his eyes. Just like Nissa, he could blink and was taught to communicate by blinking answers to questions.

This man was living in a care center when he wrote his book one eye blink at a time. A former colleague would visit him every day and patiently dictate each letter of each word. They worked for several hours every day on the project.

The writer had difficulty sleeping at night so he would stay awake and compose the next few paragraphs of the book in his mind. The next day, when the dutiful scribe arrived, he would patiently blink out the composition from memory. This went on for months.

I read the description of what it was like for him to be "locked in." I wondered if it would be like that for me, and wondered if it was like that for Nissa. I decided to go ahead and read the experiences that he described in the book to Nissa. I was a little gun shy after the first book, but hoped that something he wrote would connect with her.

"Is this what it is like for you?" I would ask her.

Sometimes she would blink "yes" and sometimes she would blink "no" and sometimes she would just stare. I supposed that sometimes there was not a yes or no answer to the question.

I tried to imagine what it would be like to be in a body that could feel but couldn't move. I imagined that I would feel claustrophobic, frustrated, scared, impatient, and trapped. I struggled to imagine the things he described. I understood the descriptions of how he perceived the world, but couldn't quite grasp the experiences he put into words.

I came to the conclusion that we are all different and would experience and cope with the situation differently. Nissa is a very patient, low-key, willing-to-accept-and-adapt kind of person. Her temperament is like Play Doh - she adjusts herself to whatever pushes against her and rarely pushes back. She is very accommodating.

The butterfly in the title of the book represented the eventual freedom the man found. He was able to draw on previous life experiences and his imagination to go on adventures in his mind. He found a way to be free and pass the time by keeping his mind active. After a while, he didn't seem to notice that his body did not accompany him on his journeys. I never did understand the "diving bell" part of the book title. He said it was how his body felt.

(In 2008 the Sundance Film Festival featured a movie based on the book, "The Diving Bell and the Butterfly". The diving bell was an old-fashioned scuba diving suit with a large round metal full head helmet. He must have felt like he was underwater while paralyzed.)

I admired his ability to rise above the confinement of his useless body. He was restless enough to be active, but not so restless that it created agitation. I don't have an imagination that could take me away like that. I'm much more practical and would need to be seeing results of some kind. I really don't know what I would do or how I would cope, but I know it wouldn't be like either of them.

I would read ahead in the book so I knew what was coming, and then read aloud the passages that I thought Nissa might connect to. Her ability to regulate emotion was impaired, so I tried to avoid triggering any tears. Once she started crying it was sometimes difficult to get the tears to stop.

The book ended abruptly with an epilog that left a lump in my throat. I felt empty even though the book had really been a tribute to a conquering spirit. I was glad to have read the book because it helped me understand a little of what Nissa was going through. I decided not to read the end to her. I came prepared with other things to entertain and engage her with.

She eventually asked the question that I hoped to escape. It came several weeks after I had quit reading the book to her so I thought I had safely moved on to other topics.

"What happened to the guy in that book?" She patiently blinked out every letter in the question.

It took me a series of yes and no questions to sort out what guy in what book but it finally clicked. She hadn't forgotten her comrade, the man who told some of her story. She wondered how it all came out.

I had decided that I would never tell her, but when the moment arrived I felt compelled to be honest.

"He died." I was forthright and to the point. "He lived less than a year after the stroke and died right after he finished the book. His friend published it for him as a tribute to him."

I went on to tell her more of the details about how the book and its author ended.

There was an awkward silence when I finished. Her eyes had a look of "oh" for a few seconds and then she drifted off.

Nissa, of course, was always silent, but after spending hours with her I could tell when she was engaged or when she had retreated to her inner world. On this occasion, she definitely retreated.

I didn't know what to say so I remained silent. Maybe she would die after a few months too and maybe that would be better than living like this. Maybe we all needed to just let go. Or maybe there was some purpose in her condition that we didn't quite understand yet. Maybe she would recover enough to become paraplegic. Maybe she would write her own story and it wouldn't look like either of the stories we had read.

I wondered what Nissa was thinking, but didn't suppose that she would tell me even if she had the energy to blink out an answer. Nissa wasn't a very verbal person even when she could talk. Translating deeper thoughts or feelings into words was not something she did before the stroke and wasn't likely to be something she would do now.

I hoped the book's ending wouldn't discourage her. At the same time, if death were part of the plan it would be good to start looking it in the eye. If she knew she was going to die she might want to dictate something to each of the girls. She might have final wishes regarding her belongings. She might want to do or see certain things one last time.

I waded in my own silent pool of thoughts and questions until it seemed appropriate to introduce another topic. I elected to leave the previous topic alone. I decided that she would need to come to whatever realization lay ahead in her own time and in her own way. As for me, I took things one day at a time and didn't look very far ahead - mostly because I couldn't see anything when I tried to look ahead.

It wasn't long after I told Nissa how that book ended that I found myself on a new quest. I had a vague memory of seeing a woman on a talk show years before. She had written a book that I thought was called "Slow Dance." She too had been totally paralyzed at one point. It took her 15 years to recover, but she finally reached a state of full recovery. She was middle aged, so the original injury would have occurred in Nissa's age range.

The memory brought me a renewed sense of hope as I told Nissa what I remembered about this story. I pledged to search for the book so we could read it. After weeks of Internet searches and visits to bookstores I gave up, but the rekindled hope lingered.

I had a strong notion that recovery was possible after all. My mind and heart shifted and I no longer had questions about the possibility of her life ending prematurely. I didn't have a vision of where it was going to end up, but had a feeling that things would move forward eventually. My "belief" was reactivated and I moved on looking for keys, clues, tools, doors, windows, opportunities, healers, or whatever I could find that would move us along.

CHAPTER 9

Afghan Angel

We were four weeks post stroke on Christmas Eve day. Excitement about Christmas was in the air at the nursing home. But the longer I stayed, the more I didn't understand why or how that excitement even got in the door, let alone be in the air.

Nissa couldn't leave her room, so she didn't see the decorations at the nurse's station or in the other residents' rooms. We had a little Christmas tree in her room and a CD player with Christmas music. We had some presents under the tree for her and the kids. We thought it would be fun for her to see the kids open a few presents. We made some simple plans to try to make Christmas special in some way for her.

I took some time to walk the halls of the nursing home that day. I looked into the eyes of those who called it home. I'm not sure why I had never seen this before, but I saw people who were incredibly lonely. Suddenly, the festive decorations on the wall were cosmetic and the background music taunting. These were forgotten souls, in broken bodies, warehoused in a place where overworked staff did their best to provide minimal care. It was a prison.

These people could not leave the nursing home or their bodies, so many chose to leave their mind and the awareness of their plight. There was only a faint hint of life in many of the eyes I looked into that day. The dismal picture plunged me into questions about our own plight.

How long could I keep coming every day and maintain my own life? How long could family and friends dutifully visit? What would it be like five years from now if she were still in this little room at the end of the hall? Would anyone come? Would her kids still know her? Would I still be this devoted? Would she become another one of those souls who only had a flicker of life left in their eyes?

The hours I spent with her that day went slowly. I couldn't find anything to talk about to pass the time. I didn't want to leave the room because I didn't want to see anymore of what I had seen earlier. It was depressing. I wanted to go home and be with my family but didn't want to leave her alone on Christmas Eve. It was another day that felt much like the one when the minister rescued us.

It was late in the afternoon when some carolers appeared at her door. They slipped into the room and a cheery spokesperson looked at Nissa and asked: "May we sing to you?"

I was excited. Live music being sung by live people; this was great! I looked into their faces, wondering who would come to a nursing home on Christmas Eve. I hoped it didn't stir too much emotion in Nissa or she would start to cry. Just about the time I expected them to start singing, an uncomfortable murmur started instead.

"Is something wrong?" I asked.

The cheery spokesperson was not so cheery as she replied, "I think we're bothering her. Maybe we should leave."

I was shocked. I stood immediately, reaching out towards them with one hand as if I could hold them for a moment.

"No, no, you're not bothering her," I tried to reassure them.

I looked over at Nissa. There she lay, unable to greet them or smile or respond to them in any way. She wasn't crying so that was good; but her blank, lifeless stare was so very hard for newcomers to understand.

Turning back to the carolers I pled, "No, please stay. She is paralyzed and can't talk. You're not bothering her. She'll enjoy your songs."

The cheery lady was now looking anxious. I couldn't tell what was disturbing her. Maybe it was that such a young woman was in such a bad way. I had overheard nursing home staff express those sentiments.

"Are you sure we are not bothering her?" she asked again.

"I'm sure," I replied hoping she would get past whatever was bothering her.

The group sang one quick carol, chanted "Merry Christmas," and moved on to the next room.

I was glad they had come but puzzled over the effect we seemed to have made on them. Maybe Nissa had had one of her spasms when they walked in. They were always disturbing to see.

I panicked a little as I realized that most people could not see past her condition to actually connect with her. She really was isolated. She needed someone to connect her to those who did not know her or understand her situation.

It was after the carolers that I started contemplating my own departure. It was a moment that I had to face. It would be one of those really difficult departures so I had tried not to think about it. I just hoped an appropriate moment would present itself and I would be able to slip out. The problem is that it always felt wrong to leave her. On Christmas Eve I figured it would feel really wrong.

My deliberation was disrupted when a woman entered the room. She had a homemade afghan in her arms. She walked directly over to Nissa's bed.

"I've made this afghan for someone. I'm searching for who I might give it to tonight." She surveyed Nissa top to bottom as she started a discourse on the making of the afghan.

I wondered how Nissa's non-responsiveness would affect the afghan lady. I was waiting for her to take a breath so I could start on my "she's paralyzed and can't talk" routine, when she turned to face me.

She wanted to know about me. I think she was trying to decide if I was trustworthy or if I would steal the precious handmade gift. She wasn't at all curious, confused, or disturbed by Nissa's presentation or condition.

She turned back to Nissa and carefully placed the afghan on the bed.

"This is for you. I made it myself. I hope it keeps you warm." Her sincerity was louder than her eccentricity.

I watched Nissa's eyes. They lit up just a little. The afghan lady chattered on a few more minutes, talking directly to Nissa. She didn't seem to notice, and definitely didn't care, that there was no response. She was confident and delighted to be giving her carefully constructed gift away on Christmas Eve.

It wasn't the gift so much but the connection that Nissa responded to. The afghan lady didn't seem to even notice the paralysis. She was excited to have the correct recipient for her gift and Nissa seemed excited to be recognized as worthy of a gift. And it all took place without me saying a word about Nissa's condition.

As the afghan lady left with a big smile on her face, I found myself fighting back tears. I was so grateful to see someone, a stranger not charged with her care, reach out and actually make a connection. A weight lifted from my heart and allowed me to let go at the end of my shift that night.

I left Nissa with a prayer that if she was lonely or needed something while I was gone that God would send another angel to minister to her. I tucked the afghan around her, kissed her forehead, and told her I would be back the next day to spend Christmas with her.

As I drove home that night and reflected on what had just happened, I was amazed by the whole event. An eccentric angel bearing a gift, and appearing at just the right time, allowed me to depart feeling at peace and left Nissa with a sense of value and worth. It was a beautiful gift, a gentle kiss from the Divine, and a memorable Christmas Eve.

CHAPTER 10

Christmas 2001

It was my little family's tradition at this stage in life to go skiing on Christmas morning. The resorts were usually open and the slopes sparsely populated. After a half-day on the ski hill, we would return home and prepare Christmas dinner.

My plan this year was to send my family off to the ski hill while I went to the nursing home in the morning. We would still do the dinner thing in the evening. I figured that Nissa's husband and children could visit Nissa in the afternoon if I took the morning shift with her.

After the visit from the afghan angel the previous night, Nissa had slept well and had a pleasant night. The new day, however, brought new challenges.

The left side of Nissa's body had never stopped having spasms since the stroke occurred. She was heavily medicated with muscles relaxants and pain medication. As the medication cocktail wore off every few hours, her body would start to curl. Her neck would curl into her shoulder, her hand would curl into a tight fist, and her toes would curl under. It looked like a full-body Charlie horse.

I sat by Nissa's side on Christmas morning trying to make small talk. It is odd to make small talk with someone who can't talk back. I'm not one who gets nervous during periods of silence, but I figured that Nissa could use a break from the silence she experienced most of the time. Problem is, I'm more of a listener than a talker; so generating small talk is work for me.

I was doing my best to chatter about nothing when I noticed the muscles in her left arm changing shapes. Her hand and wrist were strapped into a brace to prevent them from permanently curling up. I watched her hand attempting to curl under as the muscles on her arm changed formation.

"Does that hurt?" I asked as I watched it curl.

"Yes." An affirmative blink quickly followed my question.

"Have you had your medication this morning?"

Another affirmative blink was quickly delivered.

"How long ago?" I wondered if it was wearing off already.

She just stared at me. There was no way for her to answer an open-ended question with a "yes" or "no" blink. If I wanted an answer, I needed to ask a yes or no question.

I decided to check in with the nurses instead.

"Did she get her meds? What time? What dose? Have there been any changes? Has the doctor seen her this month at all? Did she get her meds last night? What time? Had she been moved this morning?" (Recent movement and long periods of time without movement were both triggers for spasms.) My questions only irritated the nurse who had no idea why things were different today. And "no," there was not an order for additional medication if it was needed.

We were on our own. The new spasms were bringing tears to her eyes and I didn't know what to do. It seemed early to be asking for another angel but we did need help, so I started to pray.

Soon, a thought came to my mind. My husband and I have some friends who have a son who has seizures. They learned of a pressure point in his thumb that would stop the seizure if they got to it early enough in the episode.

Another idea came to me. When I was pregnant I got Charlie horses in my legs that caused my toes to curl under. If I grabbed my big toe and straightened it back out, the cramp would release. I wondered if I could get her spasms to release with one or both of these techniques.

I explained to Nissa what I was up to and got her permission to proceed. First, I wrestled her thumb away from her tightly curled fist. After forcing it into a straight position, I pulled it as far away from her fist as I could.

I then turned my attention to her eyes to search for evidence that it was helping or feedback that the intervention was actually making things worse. I saw nothing in her eyes so looked back at her arm and hand.

I held this position for about two minutes and concentrated on relaxing. I didn't want any tension from my body to transfer to hers. The muscles eventually relaxed. That was exciting but I didn't know if the release occurred because of what I had done or if it just released on its own. I felt better because I was doing something besides helplessly looking on while she was in pain.

About twenty minutes later it started again. I quickly administered the "extended thumb technique" and got the spasm to release. This time the release came sooner. I assumed it was because the intervention was introduced sooner.

The spasms went on every 20 to 30 minutes the rest of the morning. We experimented with several interventions in addition to the thumb thing. I had some essential oils and the nurse brought in a heat pack. Nissa seemed to like the heat and oil combination on her arm muscles and they seemed to help ease the pain.

I stayed until the mid-day dose of medication was in her system and hoped that it would at least dull the pain if the spasms continued. I also hoped that the children would come for a visit and that she would be distracted from the pain.

I wondered why the new spasms were occurring. Maybe something was waking up inside of her or maybe something was getting worse. Or maybe she was building up a tolerance to the medication so that it was no longer effective at the current dose. Or maybe it didn't mean anything at all. Maybe it was just what was happening today and would be gone tomorrow.

Always more questions than answers.

I elected to hang on to my relearned lesson from the previous evening. God loves her and is looking after her. That felt better than other thoughts that had come to my mind as I struggled to leave her alone on Christmas Day. I knew that I needed to keep my life in balance, that I couldn't be there all the time, that I couldn't fix this, and that she had angels watching over her.

CHAPTER 11

Mischief in Her Eyes

I think it was the Saturday night shortly after Christmas when a phone call came. I had taken the two older girls for the weekend.

"I think she can move her leg," said the hesitant yet excited voice on the other end of the phone.

"Really?" My voice echoed in an excited questioning tone.

It was Nissa's husband who went on to explain that he had been at the nursing home that evening and was doing the routine range of motion exercises. Whenever any of us came to visit, we would always do range of motion manipulations with her legs and arms. Lying immobile for hours at a time compresses parts of the body that come in contact with the bed, creating a lack of circulation that results in bedsores. Once bedsores emerge, they are difficult to treat and often lead to more serious medical problems. We were sure that the nursing home did not move her very often, and did not check for bed sores often, so that was one of the routine things we did when visiting.

On this occasion, when her husband tried to move her right leg, it stiffened and he was unable to complete the routine the physical therapist had taught us. After several tries, he had the impression that this new occurrence was somehow under her control.

So he asked, "Are you doing that?"

She blinked once for "yes."

He repeated the experiment several times just to make sure.

As I listened to him describe what had happened, I could tell he was struggling to believe it.

"Will you try it with her next time you come in?" he asked.

"Sure," I answered. I had planned on taking the girls in to see her the next day.

"I'll let you know how it goes", I assured him.

"Call me."

"I will." I could tell he was deep in thought as he wrestled with what this might mean.

The next day, when the girls and I arrived, we went through the usual routine of jumping on the bed, showing Mom the pictures they'd colored, told Mom what they had been doing, looked at and touched everything in the room, and then settled down to play with something on the floor next to her bed. They didn't seem to care that Nissa couldn't respond to them and carried on as if their mother was participating with them.

There was a cache of art supplies and toys in Nissa's room for the girls to use when they came to visit. When they got bored, we would walk to the far end of the care center to visit "Mr. Eel" who lived in the aquarium at the front entrance. After counting all of the fish and waiting to see if Mr. Eel would make an appearance, we would make the long walk back to Mom's room to tell her what we had been able to see that day.

When we ran out of entertainment, it was generally a good idea to leave. Nissa was very sensitive to loud noises. They gave her a headache very quickly. So when the kids started to get loud from being bored, we usually kissed Mom goodbye and left.

I knew that I would only have a few minutes to interact with Nissa before the first fish tank excursion

The girls loved to draw pictures for their Mom. Nissa's room was decorated with art work from the children.

would need to take place. The girls would entertain themselves long enough for the experiment to be performed.

I began the range of motion routine on her legs without telling her that I had received a phone call the previous night. I was concentrating on what I was doing because it was easy to move a body part the wrong way and do damage. Suddenly, her right leg became abnormally stiff. I stared more intently at her right leg and then looked up into her eyes.

"Did you do that?" I asked while studying her eyes for a response.

The answer came first through the mischievous energy radiating from her eyes. It was a look I hadn't seen before and almost as exciting as the affirmative blink that followed.

"You are stopping me from moving your leg?" I was very specific in my question.

She blinked "yes."

"Can you move your leg if I'm not pushing against it?" I wanted to see if she had the ability to create movement on her own.

We both stared carefully at her immobile leg but it remained immobile, not even a hint of muscle tension. I searched other muscle groups for the ability to resist movement like what was occurring in her right leg, but there was no response.

I pushed again on her right leg. She was able to resist the movement when she had something to push against. She had the ability to resist but not to move. I wondered if we could build up this ability to resist to the point that it would create the ability to move. And, if she were able to create some small movement in her leg, I wondered if it could be worked into further movement.

On Monday, I made it a point to find the physical therapist and asked his opinion on our new discovery.

"It's probably nothing. Your sister is paralyzed." He was straightforward and offered no hope.

I asked if he would come see a demonstration. He reluctantly agreed. After watching our demonstration, he shrugged his shoulders, shook his head side to side, in a classic "no" motion and repeated, "It's probably nothing."

"But it's new movement," I challenged.

"Probably not," he countered.

"You don't think this means she's thawing out a bit?" I pushed a little harder.

"People don't thaw out when they are paralyzed. Not after this long." He didn't budge.

I thanked him for his time and then hoped that he would leave, which he did.

"Nissa, I say we keep working it and see what happens." I wasn't ready to give up the thought that it would lead to something.

Nissa and I developed some simple exercises that worked the resistance muscles that she had control of. We worked them several times each hour, every time I came. The resistance eventually did lead to the ability to tense the muscles in her right leg. As she tensed the muscles, her leg would move a little. Since the physical therapist didn't believe anything would happen, we were on our own to figure out what to do next.

CHAPTER 12

Carli J

Little Carli J was now two months old. She had not received our religion's traditional christening ritual where her name would be formally declared and she would be given a special blessing. Carli was quickly growing out of the newborn stage in which this ceremony is usually performed.

It was decided that we would gather a few friends and family at the nursing home and have the service conducted where Nissa could attend. We got clearance from the nursing home to use the cafeteria. Nursing staff agreed to hook Nissa up to a portable oxygen tank so her bed could be wheeled down the hall to the cafeteria.

This would be a day of firsts for Nissa: The first time to leave the room she had been in for over a month; The first time to have her hair washed in about 6 weeks; It would be the first time since the stroke to be dressed in nice clothes and have makeup on. We tried to arrange for a first bath or shower, but it sounded like there was a good chance she would be killed in the process. So we settled for the usual sponge bath.

It was Sunday, January 6, 2002. Teena and I arrived early that morning, armed with odds and ends from the house that we hoped would help us accomplish our mission - buckets, hoses, towels, and other such things we felt compelled to sneak in the back door so as not to alarm the nurses.

We started with the hair. It was long and permed and unbelievably matted from being laid on for so many weeks. It gave Nissa a terrible headache and made her instantly dizzy and nauseous when her head was moved at all. Her hair hadn't been washed since the stroke and rarely had it been brushed. It would be our most ambitious task of the day.

I brought a coiled plant watering type of hose with an adapter for the sink so I could hook it up in her room. I thought I could hold her head up and put a pan under it and then have Teena wash and rinse her hair while I held her head.

Plan A was a disaster. The hose adapter didn't work, lifting her head caused eye-popping pain, and it would take much more water than the pan would hold to get the weeks of leave-in-shampoo that had been layered on back out of her long hair. To top it off, the nurse on duty caught us and nearly kicked us out.

We eventually enrolled the nurse in our quest to make this a special day. She volunteered some suggestions, brought some extra towels, and then turned her back so she would see nothing and could claim to know nothing if something went wrong.

Plan B was not graceful but did get the job done. We put layers of towels under her head instead of her pillow and then poured water over her hair. We went through a huge pile of towels - both the ones we brought from home and the ones the nurse had given us. We were all wet and the bed had to be changed, but she had her shiny, dark, curly hair back.

We called a CNA (Certified Nurse Assistant) in to bathe her since she was all wet anyway and to put dry sheets on the bed. Changing the sheets with an immobile body in the bed was quite a feat and required rolling Nissa around quite a bit. It was very painful for Nissa and we had already tormented her significantly.

I hoped we weren't doing too much. The last thing we needed was to trigger another stroke. She had blood clots in her legs - and who knows where else - that could break loose and cause a heart attack or another stroke. She was on a regular diet of blood thinners that were supposed to be dissolving the blood clots, but there was no way to know if it was working.

We were watching the clock to see what else we could do before guests began to arrive. Nissa appeared to be tolerating all of the movement, so we went forward with the plans. Teena went to work on the makeup and I got out the new, fancy clothes.

Earlier in the week I had gone to a nice department store, bought several blouses, and brought them to her. Nissa chose the one she liked the best for the special day, and I returned the others. I carefully cut a seam up the backside of the blouse to get it ready for her.

I had started buying her clothes to wear because she didn't like being in a hospital gown day and night. Cutting a vertical seam up the back and sewing a few snaps on made dressing less painful for her and the nurses.

Basically, shirts could be put on by just laying them on her and threading her arms through the sleeves. I would usually just tuck the sides underneath her rather than bothering with the snaps. To get the snaps done up, you would roll her to one side and then wrap that side of the shirt around to her back and then roll her to the other side to bring the other half of the shirt to her back where the two halves could be snapped together. I bought her pants extra large so that it would be easier to wrestle her immobile body into them.

Given that we had just put her through quite a lot of trauma, I elected to do as little as possible with this portion of the operation. I decided to wrap her from the waist down with a hospital gown - covered with a nice blanket that Teena had given her. I then threaded her arms through the new blouse and tucked it carefully under her sides.

The final event was to have the nurse's assistant come and change Nissa's diaper and empty the catheter bag so everything in that department would be fresh and clean. I occasionally changed her diapers if I had to but preferred not to on this day. I think it was like that for me when she was born too. Some things don't change, I guess. It seemed less humiliating for Nissa to have a professional take care of that need, so I usually deferred to the staff for that reason as well.

Guests were arriving as we were exchanging the oxygen piped

in through the wall for a portable tank. The nurses put an oxygen monitor on Nissa's finger and instructed me about the range her stats should stay in.

"Aren't you going to stay with her?" I asked.

"Do you want me to?" The nurse asked in return.

"What do I do if the stats drop?" I didn't want to risk further brain damage from lack of oxygen.

"She'll be OK. Come get me if you need me." The nurse was clearly busy and needed to attend to others.

Nissa's two older girls arrived all dolled up in dresses and Sunday hair-dos. The grandma from Nissa's side of the family, Grandma Rue, had the two of them all ready for the big event.

Then the guest of honor arrived with the grandma from the other side of the family, Grandma Lou. Little Carli J. was in a long, white dress with a little white hair band around her head. She was beautiful! Carli lived with this paternal grandmother who proudly shared the little guest of honor with her mother.

We took pictures of mom and daughter, Nissa and Carli together. Mom looked great too, except for the blue trache tube sticking out of her neck. She almost looked normal with her hair clean and shiny, and with her makeup on. It was the first time many of the friends and family had actually seen her since the stroke, and everyone commented on how good she looked.

We gathered a small group of people to help wheel the bed out of her room and down the hall to the cafeteria. As the bed started moving, Nissa's eyes shot open wide and a look of horror came into them. I didn't think we had time to play the 20 questions game to figure out what was going on so I instructed that any turning movements be made gradually and that the bed be moved very slowly.

The movement may have caused a feeling of anxiety or maybe made her dizzy. She often expressed feeling dizzy when she was holding still. She hadn't really been moved much since being in the nursing home, so whatever sensation it was causing was probably fairly novel.

I talked to her and kept eye contact all the way down the hall in

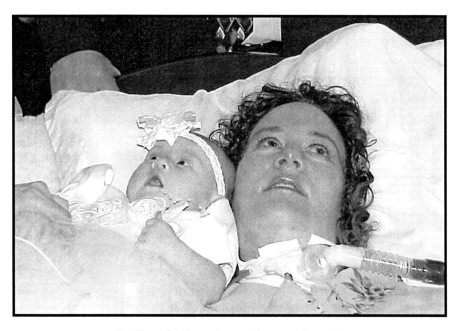

Carli and Nissa dressed up and ready.

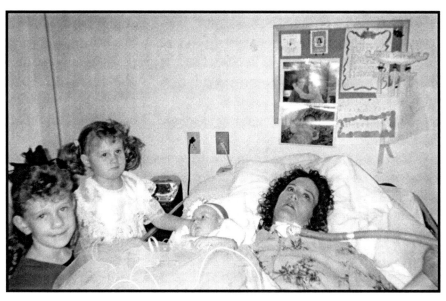

Shylee, McKenzie, Carli and Nissa all ready for the big event.

an effort to distract her from whatever she was feeling. It didn't seem to get any worse so we crept along until we reached the cafeteria door.

There were three or four rows of family and friends on one end of the room, and a couple of rows of nursing home patrons on the other end. We positioned Nissa between the two groups. The blessing was to be part of a short church service, so the nursing home patrons got to see the one and only baby blessing to ever take place in the care center.

Nissa began to cry early in the service, probably as soon as she heard the piano being played. For some reason, church music had that effect on her. Too bad we couldn't do a country and western prelude; she seemed to handle honky tonk much better.

Her crying could not be heard because of the type of trache that was attached to her throat. It didn't allow for sound. Her face, however, would move into some really odd contortions. It was clear that it was going to be one of those crying episodes that would take a long time to recover from. Her oxygen stats dropped to a really low level and stayed there. I started to get nervous about her making it through the service.

The episode of tears progressed to the point that Nissa was no longer breathing. I had her bed moved back away from the rows of people and went to work on her. Her oxygen stats remained at a really low level, so I had someone go look for the nurse as I stood over Nissa and thumped on her chest.

"Breathe, breathe, you need to breathe," I chanted as I thumped on her chest with my fingers.

I knew that she did not have control of what was happening, but I hoped to disrupt the involuntary spasms and get it to release long enough for her to get some air.

The "breathe, breathe" chant was also for my benefit so that I too would keep breathing. I have a tendency to freeze and hold my breath when I am anxious or concentrating really hard. I was breathing with every chant and round of thumps hoping that she would follow suit.

The meeting proceeded as if nothing was happening. Most of

the attendees were paying attention to the person in charge and not to our little trauma that was occurring off to the side. A nursing assistant arrived and looked helplessly on as I did my thumping ritual. The crying spasm had released a couple of times, allowing for some air and a slightly better stat reading for a second or two.

I caught the nursing assistant's attention with my eyes and motioned with my head for her to look at the oxygen monitor on Nissa's finger. She moved closer and leaned over to see the numbers. She looked back at me and shrugged her shoulders.

"Oh great," I thought. "She's going to be a lot of help."

"Is this dangerous?" I leaned over and whispered in her direction.

Her answer was another shrug of the shoulders and a look of "I don't know" in her eyes. It was clear to me that I was on my own with calling the shots and figuring out what to do.

The blessing was the first thing on the agenda for the meeting. In-between thumping her chest and telling her to breathe, I attempted to listen to the blessing and narrate it to her. I hoped to distract her and maybe start softening the crying episode. I imagined that the crying, though silent to the outside world, was causing enough internal commotion that she couldn't concentrate on the blessing and possibly couldn't even hear it.

Blake, a good friend of the family, was the one to deliver the blessing. He seemed to have a glimpse into the future and attempted to put some of what he perceived into words.

"The day will come when you will look back at this very day and treasure it as you realize and understand that as an infant your mother encountered an affliction." As he peered into the future, he addressed Carli as if she could understand him.

"When these months have passed … years … time will lapse." He struggled to bring into focus what he was sensing.

"Time will lapse … as your mother recovers." His voice was strong and certain now. "You will look back and treasure … it will cause a bond between you and your mother, a great bond."

Bonding was a big concern for those of us close to the situation. Carli had her mother 24 hours a day, 7 days a week, for the first four weeks of her life. And then in a flash, she was gone. Carli would never hear her mother's voice again; she would never be cuddled or rocked or watched over. They could see each other if we held the infant up to Nissa's face, but there was no other way to connect for the two of them.

As a psychologist who has worked with children who have had disrupted mother connections early in their lives, I was keenly aware of the possible ramifications of this disconnect. Luckily, Carli had a grandmother who could devote herself to caring for an infant and loved her as deeply as any surrogate mother can love a child.

I was intensely interested in the bonding that Blake sensed for Carli and Nissa in the future. It sounded however like it would be years away. I wondered how old Carli would be before she actually got to know mother.

As for the part of the blessing that spoke of "recovery," I didn't know what to do with that. It sounded like death was not in the cards anytime soon, but past that, I wondered what it meant. It seemed out of the question that she would ever be herself again. Maybe the slight tensing in her leg was the crack in a doorway that would open to something bigger - something beyond the nursing home that I could believe in and pray for. A new ray of hope broke through that day, but what it was shining on was not evident at all.

CHAPTER 13

Aloha in the Emergency Room

Nissa had been receiving speech therapy in the nursing home from a therapist named Tim who worked across the street at the hospital. He came over a couple of times a week to work on developing a communication system for her that involved pictures instead of words. The pictures were of daily living needs or activities. The staff was supposed to point to the pictures and Nissa would respond with the "yes" and "no" eye blinks. It was a break from the alphabet routine of spelling words one letter at a time. Tim really seemed to believe that Nissa could progress in some way and kept trying new things.

Tim suggested that Nissa's tracheotomy be downsized to a "speaking trache" to see if she could develop the ability to make intelligible sounds. The plan was to have the old trache removed at the nursing home and replaced by the new one in the same incision. No surgery necessary, it was a simple procedure.

The respiratory therapist performing the simple procedure emerged from the room with something other than victory written on his face. In fact, he looked embarrassed.

"The trache is stuck. Tissue has begun to grow over it. I'm afraid if I force it that she could bleed. I think it will have to be surgically removed. I'm sorry but I won't do it here. I think it should be done at the emergency room," he motioned in the direction of the hospital across the street.

The next day, the local ambulance company came to drive Nissa across the street to the emergency room. The charge for the five-minute excursion was five hundred dollars. It would be another five hundred for the journey back across the street an hour later when the procedure was finished.

We were tempted to just wheel her bed out through the back door, across the cross walk, and into the ER ourselves; but we were sure we would be arrested for taking property from the nursing home. We just hoped the one thousand dollars worth of rides would be worth it. It would be Nissa's first time outside in months.

The ER doctor that day became one of my heroes. He was dressed in brightly colored scrubs decorated in a tropical print. I wondered if he had just gotten back from Hawaii or something. He had a look in his eyes that said he was fully engaged in life and liked his job. After seeing that look in his eyes, I thought it was plausible that the Hawaiian print on his scrubs was a reflection of his personality.

He seemed overly interested in Nissa's situation. She was clearly more than just another wounded body to his medical eyes. He was about Nissa's age and asked a lot more questions than he needed to for the situation at hand. The conversation eventually turned to the topic of rehabilitation.

"How would we get her into Rehab?" we asked him.

"That's easy. Her doctor just needs to make a referral to the Rehab unit. She'll be screened for rehab potential and then she's in." He made it sound so simple.

I wondered: if it was really that simple, why hadn't it happened sooner, or why hadn't her doctor suggested it?

We placed an emergency call to the attending physician at the nursing home. He had only seen Nissa a couple of times since she had been admitted to the nursing home. We had never been able to speak directly to him, but sometimes could get a message to him when we were concerned about medical issues. We were surprised to get through to him this day and to have a prompt answer.

"Absolutely not. She is totally paralyzed with no rehab potential at all. She must be able to move something before she would be accepted as having any rehab potential. It is not an appropriate referral." He was firm.

We reported what we had been told to the tropical doctor in the emergency room. We also reported that she had developed some movement recently of which the attending physician was not aware.

We were still diligently working on her resistance muscles. She had developed the ability to tense up her right leg causing it to rotate ever so slightly in one direction. It wasn't much, and we didn't know if it had the potential to amount to anything, but it was voluntary, unassisted movement. We had her demonstrate it for the ER doc.

He shrugged his shoulders and said, "It looks like movement to me" as he disappeared out of the room. He reappeared a while later with a smug kind of look on his face.

"She's been accepted to the Rehab Unit." His smug face broke into a full-blown smile.

"But how?" we asked, not believing our ears.

Tim the speech therapist, who had been working with Nissa, just happened to be a part of the treatment team on the rehab unit at the hospital. For some reason, he had brought her up in staffing meeting that morning at the hospital. He told the rehab doctor about her and expressed the opinion that Nissa would never rehabilitate at the nursing home. The rehab doc put two and two together and realized that the ER doc was talking about the same patient the speech therapist had staffed earlier.

The ER doc made the official referral and the rehab doc accepted her without even seeing her. He considered the speech therapist's staffing to be the screening. And just like that, she was cleared to move on to the next adventure.

The ER doc offered to let us watch the surgery to downsize the trache. I elected to go eat lunch instead. I didn't want to risk passing out and becoming a patient at the ER myself.

The surgery was quick and uncomplicated. I studied the new trache protruding from the fresh incision in her neck. It was a different shade of blue; but other than that, I couldn't see much difference.

Now it was time for the five hundred dollar ride back. The rehab unit said they would have a bed for her the next day. Then it would be another five hundred dollar ride across the street again to check into rehab.

The ER doc overheard our grumbling about the five hundred dollar rides and went to work again. I couldn't believe he was still interested in helping. Talk about going the extra mile.

"It would be cheaper to keep her here in a medical bed than do the running back and forth," he offered.

We were speechless and just looked at him with questioning in our eyes. He got that smug look on his face and disappeared again, leaving us to guess what he was up to.

It took him a while but when he reappeared he nonchalantly announced, "There's a bed on the Rehab Unit after all."

I wasn't sure if it was the look on our faces or the fact that he had been able to pull off another miracle, but he broke into a contagious smile that melted our surprise and disbelief into laughter and grateful acceptance.

I looked deep into his eyes for just a moment as his smile lingered. I wanted to see what motivated him. I wondered what he saw in Nissa that her attending physician didn't see. I wondered why he was going the extra mile for her. I could feel that this was a turning point that had been divinely arranged. I wondered if we were on an episode of "Touched by an Angel" or something.

The moment passed and all I saw was someone who was happy to have been able to help. My curiosity about him lingered as I questioned him about the situation.

"How did you pull that off?" I asked, hoping he would tell me about his magic.

"Sometimes there *really* is no bed. And sometimes, if you yell loud enough, there really is a bed after all." He laughed as he walked away.

"Go pack her stuff. She's staying here," he hollered over his shoulder as he left the room.

For a few minutes it felt like Christmas morning. We had no idea that this surprise was coming. It was a gift that shot a ray of hope into a situation that had become dreary. There were at least two doctors on the planet that thought she could move forward and a team of professionals to help pull it off. The rehab unit sounded like the Cavalry and I was happy to hear that rescue was on its way.

We left Nissa at the ER while we returned to the nursing home to pack her things and arrange for her discharge. The Director of Nursing seemed angry and the nursing staff hurt, as if we were betraying them. One young nurse came in as we packed the room.

"Why are you taking her somewhere else?" she asked with great sincerity.

I was grateful to see that she cared about Nissa, but didn't know what to say to her. I could see the disappointment in her eyes and knew that she was taking it personally. Before I could formulate a diplomatic explanation that wouldn't injure her further, she asked another question.

"Weren't we taking good enough care of her?"

After the holidays a new crop of young, optimistic, energetic caretakers had been hired. Some of them took a special interest in Nissa and really attempted to reach out to her. This young woman was one of them.

"It's not that," I started carefully. "The rehab unit specializes in rehabilitation. A nursing home, well, it cares for people who aren't likely to get better."

"But she had therapy here too," she persisted.

"Not the kind she will get where she is going." That's what I hoped anyway. I projected a confident tone in my voice as if I knew it to be true.

The young nursing assistant quietly left. I felt bad that she saw this as a failure for the nursing home. I felt like it was a graduation that should be celebrated. But the tone as we left with Nissa's things was quite tense.

I had often wondered if or when Nissa would leave the nursing home. I had spent hours there. I knew exactly how many steps it was from Nissa's room to the fish tank at the main entrance. I had walked the halls many times with the girls when they got bored hanging out in mom's room. We had named all the fish in the fish tank and knew most of the residents living along that particular hallway. I wondered if the days would turn to years. I wondered if the girls would grow up thinking this was mom's house.

The departure day arrived unannounced. I was not prepared for the emotion that this graduation would bring. I had prepared myself to have the nursing home be the last place I would see Nissa alive since that was the medical prognosis for her. But she had left and was still very much alive.

A wave of grief washed up on the shores of my conscious mind. I paused at the door and looked up at the rose wallpaper that lined the top of the room. It was the same wallpaper that had beckoned me the day I found the empty room at the end of the hall and thought that it was waiting for her. No longer checkered with pictures from the girls, it looked much like the first day I saw it.

Memories of the many events, thoughts, feelings, fears, and lessons all passed through my mind as I stared into the empty room. I felt a need to connect with all of it one last time. When I walked out the door, I wanted to be able to close this chapter and move on.

My final exit was out the back door closest to her room. I always parked in the back. As I pushed opened the door and stepped across the threshold leading to the world outside, a memory flew into my mind.

"One day you are going to walk out those doors with me!" I can't remember why I had felt bold enough to say something like that to Nissa, but I had. I remember it kind of took me back when I said it. Now I was leaving for the last time and she was already gone. I hoped my boldness had not been a lie. Maybe someday we'd be back and would walk out the door together. Who knew what the future held? Certainly not me.

CHAPTER 14

The Road to Recovery

The Rehabilitation Unit was such a relief. The doctor saw her every day. Most of the day was structured with therapeutic activities carried out with the belief that they would make a difference. They even rigged up a way for her to call the nurses if she needed them. This was the first time Nissa had any control over initiating communication. The level of care was almost as intense as the ICU had been.

The Rehab unit was also full of surprises that sometimes startled me. It was a place that was all about believing in recovery. It was such a dramatically different approach that it sometimes seemed preposterous. Nissa went from being condemned to paralysis to being commanded to rise and walk. I couldn't believe that such a different reality existed just across the street. I felt like I could turn my attention back to my own life and let these committed professional work their magic on Nissa.

The Christmas holidays were over by then, so I focused on establishing a workable routine with my business and personal life. I decided that I needed to simplify, so I asked to be officially released from all of my responsibilities with church, and I quit my early morning exercise class and evening activities. One of the neighbors started bringing home-cooked food for my teenaged son when she realized that he had been abandoned in this whole ordeal. I gladly ate the leftovers when I got home late at night.

I started going to the hospital every other night after work. I also went in every Wednesday at noon for the weekly staffing report, and every Sunday to take her to the short hospital worship service and hang out with her for a while. There was an optimistic, devoted rehab team working with her, so I gladly took a step back to fill a more supportive role.

Rehab started with Nissa being elevated from flat on her back to 15 degrees upright. At first, this caused her blood pressure to rise and her head to pound. Within a week she was able to tolerate an upright position. To get her upright, she was strapped to a board while it was lying horizontally, and then tilted until it was perpendicular to the ground. This also was the beginning of what was called "weight bearing activities" where she learned to stand up without collapsing.

Nissa was in a wheelchair much of the day where she had to learn to sit upright without slumping over and hold her head up without a brace. She went through all of the developmental stages a baby goes through in gaining control of her body. We kept tabs to see if she would relearn the skills faster than baby Carli would learn them for the first time.

Things seemed to progress quickly as each discipline had their turn to work her over. I sometimes stayed to watch what each player brought to the recovery process. The speech therapist put chips of ice on the back of her tongue. As the melted liquid slipped into her lungs it sounded as if she would choke to death, but eventually lead to the return of her gag reflex and then the ability to swallow. I marveled that she could be taught to swallow and wondered who figured out that causing someone to choke would bring it back.

I left the room sometimes during this procedure because I was sure she was dying right in front of my eyes. She would turn red and then blue as her lungs fought to push the water back out. She would sometimes not breathe at all for long periods of time before a small gasp brought a little air back into her lungs. I felt frantic as I watched her choking and gasping. It always surprised me to see the speech

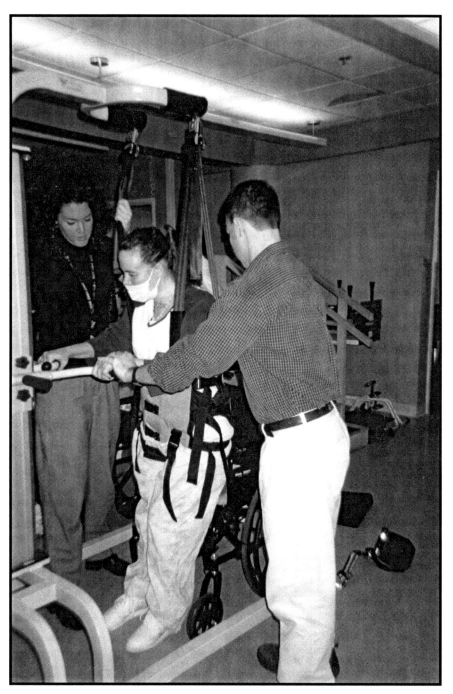

Nissa learns to bear weight.

therapist calmly observing her near-death experiences.

From ice chips, she advanced to pudding. This was the first food she had tasted in over two months. When she got the pudding to go down the right hatch by triggering a swallow reflex, life was good. When the swallow reflex was not triggered, well, let's just say that coughing up pudding is harder than coughing up water.

The next event that I happened to be there for was the peanut butter exercise. Nissa was unable to move her tongue. To encourage movement, a gob of peanut butter was stuck to the roof of her mouth. She was then instructed to touch it with her tongue. At first the peanut butter just fell, ungracefully out of her mouth. Eventually she was able to get her tongue to touch it and then move it around. I was glad she had learned to swallow consistently before starting this exercise. I couldn't imagine trying to cough up peanut butter that had slipped into her lungs.

It seemed that every day there was a new torture designed to eventually bring back a forgotten movement of some kind. Nothing came back automatically. Everything was earned through awkward, hard work from Nissa and the dedication and vision of her team of therapists. They were well on the way to defying all of the original predictions.

One Wednesday afternoon I was in Nissa's room awaiting the report from the weekly staffing. The social worker came in with a big smile on his face.

"I have some really good news," he announced.

"She's going to be paraplegic!" He said it as if it was a happy announcement, but it sounded terrible.

"The team thinks they can rehab her right side, fit her with an electric wheelchair and give her some independence." His voice was triumphant.

I stopped breathing and Nissa started crying. The new trache allowed sound to come through so her crying was quite loud now. The wailing sound alarmed the nurses who came in immediately to see what was wrong. I left Nissa with the concerned nurses and asked the social worker if he would step out into the hall with me.

"What do you mean she will be paraplegic?" There was a hint

of irritation in my voice that elicited immediate defensiveness from him.

"The team believes that she will be able to recover enough to be in a wheelchair. They think she will be able to use her right hand again." His voice had a hint in indignation.

"No one has ever told her anything about her recovery potential. She believes that she is going to fully recover. Why are you teaching her to stand if you don't think she will ever walk again? Why would you plant a limitation in her mind like this?" I was getting a little worked up as I talked.

"You are in denial!" he retorted." It is better that she understands her limitations and works with them than believing in things that are not possible. It's not healthy to let her believe in things that are not real. She needs to accept the reality of her disability and move on." He was also getting worked up.

"You don't know what her limitations will be. You guys are only guessing right now. I think it is better that she discovers her own limitations rather than having someone hand them to her. Listen to her." I paused just long enough for one of her wailing noises to reach us in the hallway and then continued.

"Do you think the news has had a positive impact on her today? Do you think that introducing an image of being paraplegic will be helpful?" I was trying hard to control my voice so as not to sound angry. I wanted to challenge him, but not disrespect his professional stance. I knew that he was just doing his job.

One of the nurses interrupted the exchange as she left Nissa's room.

"Don't you ever make her cry like that again." She scolded the social worker as she walked by us.

He took the comment, half made in jest, as an opportunity to escape. He followed the nurse back to the nurse's station and I went back into Nissa's room.

"Don't listen to him Nissa. What he said doesn't mean anything. Your rehab team is working hard and so are you. Nobody knows what is going to happen in the next two months. We just need to wait and see."

There was a tentative discharge date two months away. A lot had happened in the first month. I thought it was premature to guess what the next two months would bring, but I wasn't the expert - they were. Even if she only recovered to the level of paraplegic, I still thought it best for her to discover the wall rather than someone putting it up for her.

I wanted to be excited about the news, but instead it sent me reeling into the world of permanent disability. I tried to picture her in an electronic wheelchair like the young girl in the book we read together. Nissa wouldn't be able to live in her own home because it was multi-leveled; not a handicap-friendly home. She would not be able to bath herself or comb her own hair or care for the children.

Nissa may not be able to live at home at all. That would never do. There had to be more. I didn't want to think about it, so I put the notion out of my mind and kept looking forward for signs of recovery. I hoped her rehab team would keep pushing too. I hoped they didn't settle for paraplegic. I wanted them to believe. Believing still seemed to be making all the difference.

It was about a month later when the same social worker came in on Wednesday afternoon to report the results from the weekly staffing meeting. He kept his face as stoic as possible as he released the words, "She's going to walk out of here." He then broke into a big, genuine smile. I felt tears

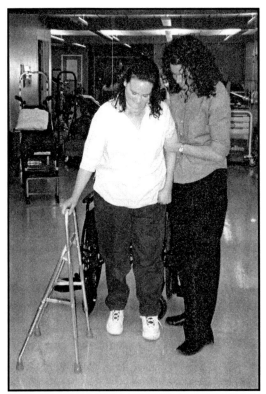

Nissa learning to walk again.

immediately spring to my eyes. I looked down at Nissa, smiled triumphantly and whispered, "I know." Her eyes twinkled and her face managed a lopsided smile in return.

Her rehab team did keep on pushing and were able to get her on her feet, supporting her own weight, and making the first gestures of walking movements. It seemed that once it was official, "She's going to walk out of here," that her walking started to take form and progress.

During that same month, she was able to start using her right hand to feed herself. She held the spoon awkwardly in a closed fist and then thrust her arm towards her face. At first, she was not able to hit her mouth with the spoon, but quickly progressed to being able to eat most of her meals unassisted. She was a mess when she was done eating, but the hope of independence and the taste of real food kept her working on those skills until she had them mastered. Once the food intake by mouth was adequate to sustain her, the feeding tube was removed. This was the first evidence of independence that shown a gleam of hope into the future.

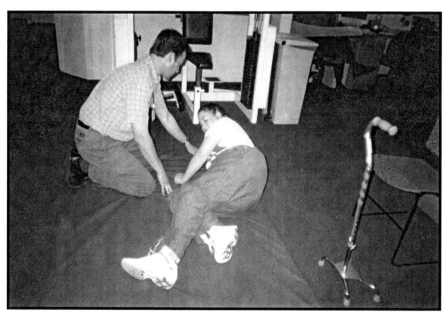

Learning to get up off the ground turned out
to be a crucial survival skill for when she fell.

CHAPTER 15

Emancipation

I'm not sure if it was for my benefit or hers, but I tried to get her out of her hospital room as often as possible when I came to visit. It was quite an ordeal, but staying in her room was an ordeal as well.

Before she had been transferred to the Rehab unit, Nissa's trache had become infected at the nursing home. The infection spread to her lungs. When her lungs got too full it would sound like she was drowning, so we would have someone come and suction them out. She was not able to cough voluntarily, but would sometimes involuntarily go into a coughing spasm. When this occurred, disgusting, green, smelly goop would shoot out of the trache tube as if it were a harpoon.

One day, an occupational therapist was moving her and the movement triggered a coughing spasm. He got splattered with the green stuff. It was beyond disgusting, but we all broke out in a fit of inappropriate laughter. He looked like he was going to cry but kept himself composed long enough to finish moving her and then quickly left, probably to scrub his face with iodine and burn his clothes.

We had a running joke about her loogie shooter after that, and were very cautious of our position in relationship to the opening in the trache tube. The humor, though inappropriate, was a necessary coping mechanism that we employed regularly.

The infection became serious while she was at the nursing home and Nissa was started on a series of antibiotics. The antibiotics were prescribed at higher and higher doses, and then switched to more powerful forms.

Nissa's catheter bag would fill with blood and what looked like blood clots. It was alarming and looked dangerous but the nurse's only comment was, "that's normal." It was virtually impossible to talk to the nursing home doctor, so we never knew what he knew or thought, or if he was monitoring her medical condition at all. All I knew was that the blood clots in the catheter bag did not look normal to me.

We were eventually told that she had MRSA (Methicillian-resistant staphylococcus aureus). That meant that she had a staph infection that was antibiotic-resistant. Her immune system would have to fight the infection because the bacteria were outsmarting the antibiotics. At the same time, she was kept on antibiotics. I asked why she was still on antibiotics if she had an antibiotic-resistant infection, but nobody would answer my question.

Our older brother, Shane, came in and gave her a blessing. In his prayer he asked for the infection to be healed. Within a few weeks, Nissa no longer had any visible signs of the infection. Her secretions were clear and there were no more green loogies shooting from the trache tube.

A sputum sample was sent to the lab when Nissa was transferred to the hospital rehab unit. It showed that she was still positive for a certain strain of bacteria. She was immediately quarantined. She continued to test positive the entire time she was on the rehab unit even though there was no visible evidence of infection.

Quarantined meant that anyone entering her room had to put on masks, gloves, and gowns that were thrown away on the way out of her room. It also meant that her baby couldn't visit at all and the older girls had only brief, restricted contact. We had all had liberal contact before when the infection was active and green, so the new restrictions were surprising and very inconvenient.

We were told that she may always test positive for this bacteria, but it may be kept in check by her immune system and so no symptoms would be evident. At the hospital, the weekly positive cultures meant that if she ever left her hospital room, she had to be put in a gown and have a mask over her face so as not to infect other people.

I wondered if any of us carried the bacteria since lots of us had frequented the nursing home when she was struggling with it. Hospital staff shuddered at the thought, but did not restrict our visits - other than the baby. They felt like the baby, at 3 months old, did not have an immune system sophisticated enough to risk further exposure.

So, visiting Nissa on the rehab unit meant suiting up with biohazard barriers and then trying to find meaningful ways to spend the time. I often opted to suit up just long enough to put a biohazard outfit on her and then escape off the unit. I could then shed my suit and we could go adventuring through the labyrinth of hallways in the hospital.

Nissa had the hallways memorized from our walks, but I managed to get lost almost every time we went out. One day, while standing at the intersection of the ER, Radiology, and Oncology corridors, I saw Nissa's head lean to one side. I walked around the wheelchair and hunkered down so I was eye to eye with her.

"Are you trying to tell me where to go?"

Her eyes immediately smiled. I didn't know if she was smiling because she had gained the ability to nod her head or because she liked the joking about telling me where to go.

"Nod your head again," I instructed.

Without much effort at all, she leaded her head ever so slightly to one side.

She had spent a whole month trying to learn how to hold her back straight and keep her head in proper alignment with her neck. She was on a boatload of muscle relaxants to keep the left side of her body from curling up in response to the spasms that continued.

At first I thought her neck was just curling like it always did but this looked deliberate.

"Nod the other direction." I wanted to see if she really had control.

She easily tilted her head in the other direction.

"Well, look at you!" I was excited.

"You can move your head. Let's see if you can keep it up. From now on whenever we come to an intersection, you nod which way you want to go."

And so off we went. Nissa was able to direct her journey with the slight nod of her head. From then on, I let her guide our tours through the hospital. I hoped this was a foreshadowing of greater control of many things in her life.

One day, when we returned to her hospital room, I couldn't find anyone to help me transfer her from the wheelchair back to the bed. It took all of her strength to sit up while we strolled through the hospital. After a while, she would lean to the side and tip over in thewheelchair. I usually headed back to the unit when she started to lean.

Transferring from the bed to the wheelchair and vice versa was tricky. I had been taught several transferring techniques, but never really got comfortable with any of them. The one that usually went the smoothest required Nissa to support her own weight on her legs for just a moment while I pivoted her from one place to another. When she was tired she couldn't do her part.

I usually tried to get a CNA to help me, but on this particular day I couldn't find anyone and she was fading fast; so I decided that I just needed to be brave and go for it. I positioned the wheelchair and put on the brakes. I eyed the bed and began a dialog out loud about what I was supposed to do. Then I readied myself for the launch.

"On the count of three. Ready. One, two, three."

I leaned her forward until her weight shifted over her feet. The pivot started out OK but then she landed too close to the edge of the bed and she and I both rolled onto the floor.

I was horrified. I'd had some clumsy and awkward transfers before, but never spilled her onto the ground like this. I was afraid that she had been hurt in the fall. I untangled myself from her and then carefully straightened her body out.

"Are you OK?" I asked with a tenderness that I hoped covered my anxiety.

She blinked reassuringly.

"I'll be right back. I've got to find someone to help get you back in bed. Will you be OK if I leave for a few minutes?"

She blinked again.

I wasn't sure if I would be in trouble with the nurse or not. I hoped they didn't ban me from taking her on excursions or require that I wait for them to do all of the transfers. They were usually busy and if I insisted on help it usually meant a long wait. I found the nurse and sheepishly explained what happened.

She came quickly to Nissa's room to assess the damage. After she determined that Nissa was not hurt, she had a CNA help her get Nissa off the floor and back into bed. Moving dead weight is a tricky feat, but the rehab team was good at it.

Once Nissa was safely back in bed, it was discovered that the catheter had been extracted during the fall. I shuddered, assuming that the extraction would have been painful. The nurse just had a discouraged look on her face.

"I really don't want to put that back in," she said.

I was surprised by her statement, but even more surprised by her contemplation about leaving it out.

"What happens if you leave it out?" I asked cautiously.

"Well, we start training her," she offered, while clearly still thinking it over.

"What do you mean by train her?" I wondered what she meant and why she had to think it over so hard.

"We could start bladder and bowel training," she answered with confidence.

Evidently she had thought it through and now had a plan, or maybe a sales pitch, for the doctor and daytime nurses that would have to buy into the plan.

"You mean she can learn to control all of that again? You mean no more diapers or tubes?" I had no idea she could recover that kind of control. I was excited until I thought it over for a minute.

"If she can learn that kind of control, why didn't anyone do this sooner?" I was confused. It seemed to me that not changing diapers would be a good incentive to move that part of rehab along.

The nurse didn't answer my question so I went on with more questions.

"How do you go about this? How do you train her?"

"We'll give her a stool softener at the same time every day and then sit her on the toilet until her bowels move. Eventually her bowels will start to move on their own at the same time every day,"

"Really!" I said with great surprise. I thought if it were that easy, maybe I would sign up for the program.

"Oh yes," the nurse was certain about the bowel program.

"Will she learn to recognize and voluntarily control the process?" I questioned further.

"Hopefully," she answered.

"How long will this take?" I wondered if it was a long drawn out process. I had visions of Nissa trying to stay upright on a toilet for hours at a time.

"Oh, she should be trained in a week or two."

"What about bladder training?" I was ready to move on to a more complicated subject.

"That's trickier. We'll have to ask her if she knows when she needs to void. If she can tell, then she'll have to ring us and we can hopefully get her to the toilet. If she can't tell, then we'll just put her on the toilet every couple of hours and see if she can learn to void voluntarily."

The hospital staff rigged up a button under Nissa's pillow after she learned to roll her head from side to side. If she needed attention she could roll her head to the side and depress the button that would call the nurses. It was wonderful for her to be able to reach out to her caretakers when she had a need. The trick here would be the availability of the staff to come when she needed to go.

"Maybe you will be able to go potty all by yourself before Carli!" I teased.

Going potty turned out to be a lot of work. Nissa had to be transferred from the bed to the wheelchair, and from the wheelchair to the toilet, and then stand long enough for someone to pull down her pants before she plopped onto the toilet seat. She didn't have the muscle control to lower herself to the seat, so it was more like falling backwards for her and required someone to help her land safely on the target. She was usually left on the toilet for a half an hour before the process was reversed and she was returned to her bed.

Surprisingly, the potty training went well and Nissa was quickly emancipated from the diapers and one of her tubes. This opened a new world of recovery. If she could take care of her own toilet needs, she would be so much more independent. I so hoped she would have the dignity of her own self care restored. It would be a long road with many more skills to master, but it would be so great if she could actually use the restroom by herself. My hopes were up.

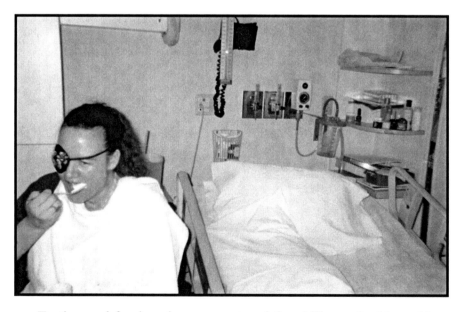

Tasting real food again was great and the ability to feed herself was a huge step toward independence. The patch is over her good eye so her compromised eye would learn to work harder.

CHAPTER 16

I'm Outta Here

The insurance company dictated when Nissa would discharge from rehab. It was not determined by her progress, but by an arbitrary date pre-selected when she was admitted. She was given three months to rehabilitate. Three months is a long time to be in the hospital, but not a long time to reinvent your body.

We were told that eighty to ninety percent of stroke recovery comes within the first three months. After that, there is a sharp plateau and not much more is gained. Nissa's recovery clearly did not fit that timetable. Her first sign of movement appeared about six weeks post stroke. We were now about three months post stroke and recovery was still clearly moving forward.

It was March of 2002 and we were headed into the final four weeks at the hospital when the rehab team decided that Nissa was capable of walking. The staff started talking about post discharge plans. It was not clear if she would discharge in a wheelchair or walking.

Because she was capable of standing and taking a few steps, the insurance company would not pay for an electric wheelchair so a manual wheelchair was ordered. The staff thought her house should be made wheelchair accessible because she was likely to be primarily in a wheelchair.

One day after the weekly staffing meeting where going-home plans were discussed, the social worker emerged as usual with a report.

"Everything is looking good except for him." The social workers voice was matter of fact.

"Who?" I was at a loss in the conversation already.

"Her husband. He's the weakest link." The social worker volleyed the information to me and waited to see what I was going to do with it.

I felt defensive but tried to control my voice so as not to reveal my feelings.

"Why do you say that?" I asked carefully.

"He's uninvolved, disinterested, and distant. We're concerned about him," he continued.

"Have you tried inviting him in?" I challenged.

"If he were involved in her recovery, he would be here. We can give him a call, but the weakest link generally stays the weakest link." He delivered the message with resignation in his voice.

It wasn't the first time I had heard these sentiments in one form or another from staff. I didn't want to think about it, so I chose to stay in denial and hoped that they were wrong. I knew deep down that if they were right, there wasn't anything I could do about it; but I still just hoped that they were wrong.

Nissa had not been home for three and a half months. Her middle daughter's fourth birthday was coming up. I asked if Nissa could go home on a pass for the day, but was told that the insurance company figured that if you are well enough to go out on a pass then you are well enough to go home.

I didn't know how the insurance company would know she was out on pass and felt strongly about the whole topic for some reason. I decided to write the doctor a letter explaining the therapeutic benefits of a pass for a few hours and promised that it would be the only request prior to her release. He granted the pass.

I found a t-shirt with the cartoon character "Taz" on it that said, "I'm outta here." It made Nissa smile. We planned a simple party with close family members and had our first adventure outside the hospital. Nissa was thrilled to be home for a few hours and looked around as if she was seeing it for the first time.

She was able to hold her baby for the first time in months and feed her a bottle. Nissa was able to feed herself by then too, so she enjoyed pizza and birthday cake unassisted. It was very encouraging seeing her in her home doing normal activities instead of rehabilitation exercises.

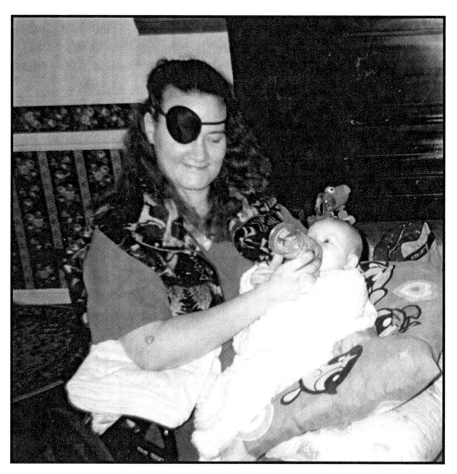

Nissa feeding Carli on her outing away from the Rehab Unit.

I tried to imagine her at home permanently. It felt hopeful. There was still one month of rehab to go. Maybe she could gain enough in the next four weeks to fend for herself when she returned home.

The weakest-link comment was in the back of my mind. Nissa's husband was hard to read. He went through the motions of being involved that day, but showed little emotion. He appeared overwhelmed, but that seemed appropriate given the circumstances. I just hoped they were all wrong about him.

When the big discharge day arrived, I stayed in the background so her husband could step up to the plate. He took the day off work and attended the discharge meetings with her treatment team. I also took the day off and packed up the room she had spent three months living in.

At this stage in her recovery, Nissa was not able to walk on her own, and needed help transferring from wheelchair to bed, wheelchair to toilet, etc. Basically, she could not be left alone and could not care for herself. Her home was a split-level, with stairs in every direction that presented significant obstacles. Nissa ended up spending most of her time in a downstairs family room where there was a bathroom nearby.

Our mother came up and spent the first two weeks at home with Nissa. After that, her husband arranged for his older daughter from a previous marriage to come help out in the mornings. Nissa spent the afternoons at the hospital in an intensive outpatient rehab program. Neighbors took turns giving her rides to and from the hospital for her daily outpatient care.

This routine went on for about six weeks until it was decided that she would go live with our mother in the southern part of the state about five hours away. Mom developed her own therapy routine that included walking, climbing stairs, and working on hand and wrists movements that would eventually lead to self-care activities. Nissa also continued in physical therapy with professionals several times a week.

After about 6 weeks of intense Mom therapy, Nissa went home again. It was the end of June and she was seven months post stroke.

She continued to attend outpatient physical therapy for several more months and then switched from professional therapy to going to the gym with her friend, Connie.

Nissa lived at home for about a year. During that time, the children were often with their grandmother who lived a few miles away. Her husband tended stayed away until late at night, and then said it was too late to go get the children from his mother. Sometimes weeks would go by between times that Nissa would see all of the children. She was left at home, alone, for long periods of time, but seemed to manage to take care of her basic needs.

I generally called once or twice a day to check on her, although she was very difficult to understand on the phone. We also emailed when we needed to communicate longer or more complicated messages to each other. I tried to make it over every Saturday to help grocery shop and do house work. It was disturbing to see the stacks of unopened mail piling up on the counter. The kids were rarely there and the house had a cold, empty feeling.

Their marital relationship gradually deteriorated to the point that he demanded that she leave or he would file for divorce. He said he needed a break. She did not want a divorce, so she acquiesced to his demands. He wanted her to go to her mother's to live. That would put her five hours away and where she would not be able to see the children. Not being a part of the children's lives was unacceptable. After all, that is what she lived for- to be their mother. We searched for an apartment where she could be close to them but could not find anything she could afford. That is when she first came to live with me.

In 2003, the year that followed, Nissa worked hard to maintain a connection with the children, traveling by bus across the county to see them several times a week. The marital relationship remained distant, as it had been since the stroke. Nissa focused her energy on gaining more mobility and independence. She forged ahead believing that things would turn out okay in the end.

CHAPTER 17

The Scooter

Mobility was a problem. Nissa couldn't walk very far and was wobbly. She fell often, leaving her bruised and with an occasional broken bone. She wasn't able to maneuver the wheelchair on her own very well, so she had little independence even on wheels. The insurance company would not pay for an electric wheelchair because she was able to walk some.

I began to visualize her being able to get around on her own. I pictured her shopping for her own groceries, going for a walk with the kids, and being able to choose activities without being dependent on someone else. I began to imagine her life with more independence and freedom.

"Nissa, what would you think about getting an electric wheelchair?" I thought that it might be worth paying for somehow, even if the insurance company wouldn't help.

All I got in answer to my question was a blank stare, so I explained why I thought it might be a good idea.

"Let's go on the internet and look," I suggested to see if she was interested enough to at least look.

She agreed, so we looked through some cyberspace advertisements and discussed the pros and cons of each model we found. It was during one of the cyberspace shopping episodes that we came across electric scooters.

"That is what I want." She was definite in her declaration.

"Why?" I didn't understand why a scooter would be more interesting to her than a wheelchair.

"I don't want to feel handicapped. On a scooter, I would feel more normal. The wheelchair makes me feel handicapped." She was very clear in her explanation.

I kept my mouth shut as my mind started to commentate on her position. *"But you are handicapped and you probably will be for a long time, maybe forever. How can you feel normal? What are you thinking?"*

Luckily, I have the ability to edit before speaking and started a counterargument with my original position. *"If a scooter makes her feel better, why should I care? If it restores a feeling of normalcy and gives her some independence, then why not?"*

This was not the first time that my skepticism, which I thought of as realism, came face to face with her optimism - which sometimes felt like naiveté. I struggled to find a verbal response that would not reveal my feelings at the moment. After all, she had a right to keep believing. Refusing to accept that she was disabled might be what kept her moving forward.

I had let the chatter in my mind rattle on for longer than what was an appropriate amount of time to be silent in a conversation. I finally put together something that I thought would be appropriate to leave my lips.

"So, you would rather have an electric scooter than an electric wheelchair?"

She quickly nodded and said "yes" at the same time. She was sure about this.

The wheelchairs were more compact and looked easier to transport, but if she wanted a scooter then we would get a scooter.

I decided to have her pick out what she wanted and then we would sort out financing it. The insurance company would not pay for a scooter either, so that option was ruled out. I had spent thousands of dollars of my own money on doctor's bills, alternative medicine, massages, nutritional supplements, etc. I was willing to spend thousands more if that is what it would take to buy her this higher degree of independence, but something inside restrained me.

As we shopped and narrowed in on a scooter, I began to talk to family members about it. I think it was our mother who suggested that there may be family and friends interested in helping out with the financial end of this project.

A plan quickly took shape. An email was composed describing how an electric scooter would improve Nissa's life. A request for donations from anyone interested in contributing was attached with instructions as to where to send the donation. The email was sent out to everyone we thought might be interested in helping out.

Within a week, money and cards started trickling in. It was not unusual for me to cry as I read the words that came with the money. I didn't realize that she, or we, had so many supporting us with their thoughts and prayers. I didn't know that Nissa's journey had affected others so deeply. Their encouraging words were like wind in our sails.

Most people sent ten or twenty dollars. It would take a lot of people at that rate to add up to what we needed. I assumed that I would need to make up the difference since this whole thing was my idea to begin with. I decided to give the collection project one month and then I would place the order.

At the end of the month, the money added up to five hundred dollars. It was not nearly enough to purchase the scooter. I wondered if the boatload of kindness that came with the money was really what was needed at this point. I accepted the outcome of the project and began to look at my own finances to see what I could do to put the deal together. Then one day a letter from one of our stepbrothers arrived.

Our mother had remarried after our father died. Our stepfather had seven children and we had six children. Between the two of them, they had a lot of grandchildren and a few great grand children. The newly formed tribe rarely got together because there were just too many of us. We were, however, happy to get better acquainted with the stepfamily when we happened to cross trails at holidays or family events.

I usually leave Nissa's mail in a stack for her to sort through. I think she is on every mail-order list known to man and generally has an impressive stack of catalogs and junk mail. Carefully flipping through catalog pages occupies a few minutes of her long days with nothing to do.

On this day, I lingered after my delivery announcing that she had received another card. It was from one of the stepbrothers. I was hoping she would be as curious as I and open it while I was still standing there. The stepbrothers were all friendly with us, but we had not had the kind of experiences that create an emotional bond. I thought it was kind of him to take the time to send a card.

Nissa got the hint and struggled to open the envelope without destroying the card. If an envelope was not tightly sealed, she could sometimes get her index finger in the corner and rip it while stabilizing it with the same hand. Sometimes she could position her paralyzed hand on the envelope and it actually would stay there long enough for her to use her non-paralyzed hand to open the mail. Often her paralyzed hand and arm would spasm because of the movement, coil back to her body, and be of no use to her at all. Sometimes she could hold an envelope in her good hand and carefully tear it with her teeth.

That day I was not patient enough to watch her go through her repertoire of techniques so I just asked.

"Do you want me to open it for you?"

She nodded "yes," so I carefully opened the envelope and handed her the card. She opened it and a folded check fell onto her lap. She would have had to put the card down to pick up the check so I picked it up for her but didn't look at it. I thought it only proper for her to be the first to read the card and see the check.

Nissa squinted and closed her left eye so her right eye could focus. She carefully read the note and then handed it to me. I traded her for the check. As I began to read the note, I heard her make a noise that I couldn't easily interpret. I looked down at her to see her looking up at me with a shocked look on her face.

"What?" I asked puzzled.

"Look," she responded, handing the check up to me.

I took the check and started to survey it by scanning from left to right, searching for the reason for her surprise. I did a double take as I reached the right hand side of the check.

$1,000.00

I counted the zeros and examined the decimals to make sure I had it right.

"A thousand dollars! Whoa!" I exclaimed as I looked back at Nissa."

"Yeah," she affirmed my surprise.

"That is about how much more we need to order your scooter!"

A big smile crept over my face. I was amazed that such a large amount would turn up at the last minute. Another little miracle!

"Let's get it ordered - today!"

I went back to my room where I stored the check collection. I got a calculator out and added up where we were. With tax and shipping, we were within twenty dollars of what it was going to cost to have the selected scooter with desired accessories shipped to us. I couldn't believe it!

The scooter came within two weeks. We took a picture of Nissa on her new blue scooter and sent it along with a thank you card to everyone who contributed to its purchase.

The scooter has allowed her to keep up with the kids as they play outside. She has become the pitcher on the family baseball team. She plays crochet in the yard, shops, races bicycles, and is the favorite lap to sit on when outdoor outings are tiring. The mobility and independence has allowed her to feel more whole and be more versatile in her activities.

We are all quite fond of the scooter, but have resisted giving it a name. It is part of the family, kind of like a favorite pet with a purpose. The keys are kept in a secure location to ensure that unauthorized drivers do not joy ride without the owner. The kids love giving Mom a ride on her scooter!

CHAPTER 18

Papa's Present

Nissa rode the Paratransit bus across the valley every Monday and every other Friday to be with her oldest two children after school. Nissa had wonderful neighbors who would pick the girls up from their grandmother's house and bring them to her. She would cook dinner and hang out with them until their father got home from work and then take the Paratransit back across the valley to our home. She was not able to see Carli, her youngest, much at all. Nissa was not able to adequately care for Carli, so she stayed with her grandmother. The twice-a-month weekend visits were extra special because Nissa got to be with Carli too.

Aunt Teena left work early every other Friday afternoon to pick up all three of the girls for the weekend visit. The day before this particular visit, Nissa had received a call from her husband. He said he would be sending something with Teena when she came to pick up the girls. He gave no indication of what he was sending, but did say that he wanted to talk to her about it.

The girls were aware that their father was sending something to their mother and grabbed it from Teena as they exited the car. They ran excitedly toward their mother yelling, "Mama, Mama! Papa sent you a present!"

Nissa was sitting in her wheelchair at the end of the driveway watching for them to arrive. They quickly surrounded her, tossed the present in her lap, and watched anxiously as she struggled to get it open.

Nissa held the 9x12 inch envelope in her non-paralyzed hand and attempted to rip it open with her teeth without ruining the contents. It was a slow process, but the children patiently waited. They seemed genuinely curious about the present from their Papa.

I chose to stay at a distance so as not to interfere with the moment they were about to share. I had fleeting suspicions about what the surprise might be, but pushed them out of my mind. I decided to just be in the moment too and hoped that I would be pleasantly surprised.

Nissa wrestled the papers out of the envelope with her one good hand. She then brought them up close to her face, squeezed her left eye shut, and squinted with her right eye until she could get it to focus. The ocular muscles on the left side were still paralyzed so her eyes couldn't focus automatically. In general, the world was blurry and she saw double in her peripheral vision. Reading required some interesting gymnastics with her eyes that she was not able to sustain for very long.

She focused long enough to read the title of the document. Tears immediately started to roll down her face. The tears quickly deepened to a gut-wrenching sob. I hadn't heard her cry this way since her husband had demanded that she leave their home.

"Mama, what did Papa give you? Don't you like his present? What is it Mama? Why are you crying?"

The excitement quickly turned to questions, and then confusion, for the innocent little eyes that looked on. I could tell it would take some time to get this bout shut back down, so I whisked the girls into the house. I didn't want them to be exposed to her pain or to take it on in any way. I didn't know how to answer their questions about Papa's present, so I enlisted Uncle Lumpy's help in distracting them with something so I could get back to Nissa.

I asked Nissa if I could see the papers that she was holding. My heart sank as I read the title: "Verified Divorce Petition". I felt sad for Nissa and knew that it would break her heart. I wasn't surprised that he wanted a divorce, but was shocked that he sent the papers with the children. And I was angry that he didn't give her the courtesy of a conversation before the special delivery.

I asked Nissa if she wanted me to read it to her. She was still crying, but I thought that if she was trying to listen, she might be able to stop. She nodded "yes," so I started to read. The words seemed to just open the wound deeper and her sobs grew so loud that I was sure that she couldn't hear me or concentrate on what I was saying. I eventually just read it silently, thinking that I could paraphrase it when she got the tears under control.

I had never seen a divorce document before, so it was new to me. I didn't know the legal rules of the divorce game, but what I read left me uneasy.

"The Petitioner (him) is a fit and proper person to be awarded the sole physical care, custody, and control of the minor children. The Petitioner is entitled to child support but will waive the same due, as long as the Respondent (Nissa) agrees to the terms and provisions of this petition and subsequent Decree of Divorce. Should the Respondent (Nissa) not adhere to the Decree of Divorce, the Petitioner would be entitled to child support from the Respondent since the date of the Decree of Divorce."

Nissa was expected to give up all of her parental rights and if she didn't agree, she would be charged child support. It sounded kind of like, "you will do what I say, or you will pay".

I read on and found the "you will obey or you will pay" theme repeated several times in the document. It was clear that he had decided what he wanted and had a strategy to get it. He expected to her walk away from everything that was important to her including her marriage, her home and her children, or "pay." The document clearly did not address the children's needs or Nissa's legal rights.

When I finished reading it, I looked directly into her sad eyes and said, "I think we better get you an attorney."

Her head bowed and the tears continued. I stood by her side at the edge of the driveway where she had been waiting for the children to arrive. Her body heaved with out-of-control sobs. It felt like a dam had broken, releasing flashflood proportions of pain.

I thought it best to let it gusher out before trying to help her patch herself back together.

I went back into the house and asked Tim to take the children for a ride. I then called our Bishop and asked if he could stop by later that night to give her a blessing. When she started to look exhausted from the prolonged expulsion of emotion, I felt an urgency to help her wind it down.

I tried everything I could think of. The stroke left her emotional "on and off" switch impaired so it was challenging at times like this to find a way to shut it off. The trick that finally worked was an insulting remark about the "Petitioner" that made her laugh. Once she started laughing, she was eventually able to move herself from laughter to calm.

Our Bishop had been at an activity that night with the teenagers from our church. He stopped at our house on his way home. He gently laid his hands on her head and prayed that she would have the strength to face this adversity in her life.

Blessings usually triggered tears in the beginning, but were always comforting to Nissa in the end. This occasion was no different. Tim thanked the Bishop and saw him to the door while I attempted to help Nissa divert the tears again.

The children played in another room and acted as if everything was business as usual. I worried about how Nissa's raw pain, clearly initiated by Papa's present, would effect them. I assured them that Mama would be okay. Uncle Lumpy did what he could to keep them upbeat until they were ready to crawl into bed.

Nissa and the three girls shared one small bedroom. One of the girls always slept with Nissa. They took turns being close to her in that way. It seemed to bring them great comfort to be near her while they slept. By bedtime, life was calm again and sleep was welcomed.

It was about two weeks later when the girls bounced into the house for a weekend visit.

"Guess what, Mama?" One of the girls had some news she was obviously excited to share with her mother.

"What?" Nissa replied.

"Papa has a new friend that's a girl and we spent the night at her house!" She was excited to share the new adventure with her Mom.

"Well," I thought, "That explains the timing of the divorce papers."

I kept my thoughts to myself while carefully watching Nissa. It was like watching a sucker punch come out of nowhere and I expected another avalanche of tears to shake loose.

"Oh, really," Nissa responded.

She looked stunned but kept her composure as her daughter recounted the details of the "sleepover" that included Papa sleeping with his new friend.

I was relieved to see that Nissa was able to sustain her poise given that it must have felt like salt in a fresh wound. Nissa's girlfriends had suspected that he was having an affair. Nissa elected to deem him as a man with integrity, just going through a hard time. That was until the news of his betrayal came through the innocent lips of his children.

I was afraid that this news would reopen the divorce papers wound, but it seemed instead to seal the scab over the healing injury. It seemed to bring some closure to any questions or second thoughts.

As it turned out, the divorce papers had been signed by an attorney but never filed with the court. When Nissa did not agree with the terms in the divorce petition,(for him to have complete custody and control of the children) he put a modified divorce petition together, moving the marital debt to her (you will pay). He then filed for divorce on their tenth wedding anniversary.

Carli and Nissa celebrating Carli's first birthday
(1 year post-stroke).

CHAPTER 19

The Funky Farm House

Nissa and the three girls had been snuggly packed into a small bedroom in our home. She wanted to fight for custody of the children. Divorce was one thing, but the new move to sever her from the children had awakened a warrior in her. She was not going to accept his decision to keep the children and restrict her relationship with them without a fight.

It was apparent to Tim and I that if we were to stay in our current role that it would be in everyone's best interest to have more space. We discussed moving to the north end of the county where Nissa would be closer to the girls. Tim travels a lot and it would put him closer to the airport. It didn't really matter to me since I was commuting to work anyway.

We searched the Internet for listings, went on Sunday afternoon drives and after-work scouting expeditions, but could find nothing that looked or felt right. We then started searching the south end of the county where we currently lived. It didn't make as much sense because it clearly would not be as convenient as a north location. The searches in the south end of the county felt better, almost like we were playing the "warm, cold" guessing game. And when we were in the south end of the county, we were getting warmer.

We eventually tuned into a few locations that we felt good

enough about to take the children to see. Tim and I would go first to tune into our own reactions to the property, and then we would schedule a time to come back with Nissa and the children. We carefully watched the kids as they looked around and interacted with the yard and house. We then watched Nissa maneuver through the house to see how handicap friendly it was for her.

We found some properties we liked, but nothing that really felt right. Then one night when I was cruising the Internet, I found a listing. I can't say it caught my eye; it was rather odd looking and unattractive in the picture. The description was intriguing because it was unusual, but I can't say it was inviting. After my initial Internet encounter, I was left with a nagging feeling that I should call the realtor.

I ignored the feelings. I was tired of looking and didn't want to waste the energy on a property just because it was intriguing or unusual. When the nagging feeling intensified, I decided to call to arrange a quick walkthrough so I could cross it off the list. The realtor was a charming woman with a British accent whom I immediately took a liking to. She had a gleam in her bright eyes that hinted of mischief. She was incredibly patient as I worked through my layers of reaction to the house.

The original part of the house was built in 1896. It still had the six-inch wooden baseboards common in turn-of-the-century homes. It also had a slightly musty sort of smell unique to older homes. Other portions of the home had been built and updated during various eras of the last century.

The current owner was a contractor and had spent his weekends for the previous seven years adding on some marvelous new features. He had not been able to complete his add-ons before deciding to sell the home. The lived-in part of the house needed updating and the new part of the house needed to be finished. It had "projects" written all over it.

I think it was the sunken toilet in the upstairs bedroom that first elicited my "that's funky" comment. As we traveled through the house, there were a few other features that called forth the same declaration. My British hostess finally worked up the nerve to ask.

"What does funky mean?"

"Funky?" She had me there. How do you explain funky?

"Is funky good or bad?" She was trying to determine my reaction.

"I can't tell yet," I answered with great honesty.

I thanked her for her time and left the whole encounter with mixed feelings. The house had plenty of bedrooms and bathrooms for everyone to live comfortably. The three acres that hosted the unusual dwelling was inviting. The backyard had an ambience of peace that felt instantly soothing.

The inevitable projects however made me tired to just think about. We didn't have the time and wouldn't have the money for the kinds of projects it would take to make it feel like home to me. That's if we could line up the financing for the additional debt we would incur by buying a larger home with acreage. It seemed like a long shot and a lot of work to me.

When I walked away, I wanted to just forget about it. It was too much work and too much money. A few days went by when I started thinking about it again. It felt like something was calling me back. I felt it strongly enough that I scheduled another appointment to see it. This time I took Nissa and the girls.

I couldn't believe the children's response to the house. They were immediately animated and immediately at home. The house is a labyrinth and rather intriguing to explore. The girls ran from room to room, delighted by the nooks and crannies and unique features in each room. The crown jewel was the purple bedroom upstairs, built especially for the little girls who lived there before. The house was definitely a hit.

When we finally made it to the backyard, a temporary hush feel over the three young explorers.

"Look, it's a forest," one of them finally exclaimed.

Two rows of very tall trees stand like guardians just outside the back door. They shade the big back lawn in the morning and the two-story house in the afternoon. The girls ran through the wooded backyard touching every tree as they raced past it. They acted like they were in an enchanted forest, alive with mystery and anticipation.

Their reaction was dramatically different than any other place we had visited and unmistakably positive.

The home was well suited for Nissa's needs. There was a main floor bedroom with an attached bathroom. The kitchen and laundry were on the main floor with easy access for her. She would not need to maneuver stairs for her daily routine.

I was so taken by the children's reaction that I didn't notice the "funkiness" of the house any more. It seemed more quaint and charming this time through. I knew it would still need some help before it would feel like home to me, but I started to see it through a different set of eyes. I slowly gained a vision of how to make it mine.

The month that followed was like one of those tube slides at a water park. We moved rapidly through a series of events we did not anticipate which, in the end, plunged us into a new life. Tim's employer asked him not to travel for the month, leaving him unusually available for the many meetings, decisions, and signatures required. A creative mortgage person figured out a way to work a refinance on our current home that would free up equity for a down payment on the home we were purchasing. Before we were even sure we wanted the house, we found ourselves signing the papers that would make it a done deal.

The whole arrangement was something I swore I would never do. I would never put myself in a position of having two mortgages. I would not buy a fixer upper. I would never go into more debt than my income alone could handle. I would not buy a bigger house and go more deeply in debt when I was close to having my previous home paid for. It was odd that so much of the deal was against my grain and yet, I felt so peaceful about it. It has turned out to be one of the best decisions of my life, made primarily from my intuitive side and not my logical side. We love our funky farmhouse and are quite at home in it.

The funky farm house's backyard.

CHAPTER 20

The Threshold Guardian

Nissa asked me if I would take her to a class one evening that was being held at the church. The presenter was author and publisher Lee Nelson. I don't remember what the presentation was about, but one of the concepts he discussed turned on a light inside of me. It facilitated a paradigm shift- a cognitive reframing that helped me to cope with the hardest part of the journey that I was on with Nissa.

Visitation issues had become a monthly drama. Nissa frequently had to debate her right to have time with the children. She was portrayed to the children as "forcing" them to see her. This, and other parental alienation maneuvers, emerged and brought alarming challenges to Nissa's already-limited relationship with her children. Nissa's world revolved around the moments she got to spend with her girls. She loved being with them and playing with them and cooking for them and planning special outings for them. It didn't seem right that she would have to fight for those precious moments.

The divorce was being drug on and on. And if Nissa ever expressed an opinion or feelings that differed from her estranged husband, she would be subject to criticism, sarcasm, disrespect, and blasts of toxic rage. I was often shocked and angered by his reaction to her attempts to present her point of view.

Having someone you love suffer is tough to watch, much more difficult sometimes than going through your own trials. Nissa seemed vulnerable and ill equipped to take on the emotional and legal battle over parental rights when she was still immersed in recovering her physical abilities. It sometimes seemed just plain ill intended and mean. As her primary advocate in life, I was constantly juggling my own emotional reactions to the situation while trying to help her sort out what to do to protect her relationship with the children.

That night at the presentation, Lee discussed the Jungian concept of "threshold guardians." A threshold guardian is someone or something that guards the way to the next stage in one's development. This person or event makes you struggle or seduces you to take the path of least resistance. It proves that you are strong or it wears you down- enticing you to quit and just stay where you are.

A threshold guardian may be an enemy, a hardship, an obstacle, or an unexpected fortune, a lucky break, or advancement. The threshold guardian, be it a person or a situation, presents you with the opportunity to evolve. How you deal with the guardian determines the direction of your evolution.

I thought the stroke, with poor prognosis of recovery and all of the leftover hardships, was Nissa's big challenge in life. But as I listened to Lee talk that night, I had an epiphany.

Nissa was still very vulnerable and unable to advocate for herself in many ways. It was easy to manipulate and take advantage of her. Her emotional defense system had been wiped out and left her with an innocent-feeling emotional surface; so much so that when people met her for the first time, they often approached her as if she were a child. Just like with her physical skills, she was starting over to develop emotional skills and defenses.

What came into focus for me that night was that she needed to face the classroom bully, junior-high rejection, the pain of defeat, the uncertainty of self, the cruelty of the human pecking order, and all of the other negative life experiences that help us to build an effective emotional defense system. Like an immune system, once you get exposed to negative emotional experiences, you automatically construct a defense system to handle them.

This situation, packed with intense conflict, was providing her with a great deal of negative emotional experiences that revolved around the only thing in her life that she cared enough to fight about. Endangering her relationship with her children was a deep enough threat to reawaken her own protective instincts.

It was the perfect threshold guardian. Close enough to her heart to cause the kind of pain that toughens you up, and with enough power to truly threaten her relationship with her children. I don't think any other circumstance could serve the purpose as well as this threshold guardian did.

I ponder this new perspective, every time I am tempted to feel angry. One day as I was struggling to shift back into the new perspective, a story that I had heard years ago came to my mind.

A little boy once found a cocoon and brought it home for safe keeping knowing that the enclosed creature would eventually emerge as a beautiful butterfly. Each day he watched until the magical day arrived when signs of life began to appear. The creature inside began to flutter. This was exciting to the boy who had patiently waited. Eventually the fluttering turned to flapping as the butterfly beat furiously against the cocoon that enclosed it. The butterfly would flap until it was exhausted and then it would stop.

The boy became worried that the protective cocoon was now the very thing that would prevent the butterfly from emerging. The boy watched as the butterfly tried again and again, with all its might, to break free of its prison. The boy had waited long and patiently to see the butterfly, and was determined to have it succeed; so he began to unravel the cocoon from the outside to make it easier for the butterfly to escape. He carefully unwrapped the layers of the cocoon until his fingers met the delicate wings of the beautiful creature.

Finally the butterfly stepped out of the cocoon and stretched its wings for the first time. The boy smiled with delight as the butterfly instinctively began to rhythmically move its wings. The delicate wings fluttered rapidly in the air but were not able to lift the creature into flight. The butterfly beat its wings again and lifted off a little, but quickly fluttered to the ground where it eventually died. It did not have the strength to fly and could not survive on its own.

The boy's effort to "help" ended up "handicapping" the butterfly instead. The butterfly needed to beat its wings and struggle against the cocoon until it was strong enough to break free on its own. Only then would it be strong enough to fly.

The story reminded me that I needed to let Nissa struggle. This was her battle to fight so that she would have the strength she needed to move forward in this new chapter of her life. There was really nothing I could do but watch and wait for her to emerge. And when watching the struggle is too hard, I've learned to direct my attention to envisioning her as a beautiful butterfly with the strength and grace to make her own way through life.

CHAPTER 21

Barnyard Antics

Shortly after moving to the funky farmhouse, we started collecting a variety of farmyard creatures to populate the three acres that came with it. I've not been around farm animals enough to know what it is like to live with them. Getting to know them has been very interesting and has taught me a lot about why people act the way they do.

Our first acquisition was a horse. I was skeptical about having horses when we discussed it as an option. We had horses at our previous residence, but it didn't last long and it didn't work out very well for us.

One day as I was driving home from work, I noticed a pasture with a sign in it that said, "horses for sale." I glanced over to see a field with "paints" (pinto horses) in it. Tim liked paints because of the interesting patterns of color on them. We went back over to look that same night after dinner.

Tim liked what he saw, so we arranged a visit to the farm for the following Saturday to take a closer look. The owner brought a young, green broke (still learning what people wanted but hopefully won't throw you out of the saddle), black and white paint into the arena for us to handle. The owner was more than a little nervous as I hoisted myself into the saddle and announced that I was an inexperienced rider.

She watched carefully as the inexperienced ridee and the inexperienced rider struggled to get around the arena. The horse was a two-year-old gilding who was really not sure what he was supposed to be doing. He plodded around in a docile enough manner that I felt safe on his back.

After a few laps around the arena, I climbed back down from the saddle and announced, "I like him." He was a gorgeous horse, so I even enjoyed looking at him. He had obviously been around people and was friendly and engaging as we stood next to him.

"What's his name?" I asked as if that had something to do with his value.

"Second Chance," the owner replied.

The name hit the same chord in Tim as it did in me, and we instinctively looked away from the owner and directly at each other.

Second chances were what our lives were all about just then. Everything in our world was starting over: different house, different lifestyle, young family, new neighborhood, etc. His name symbolized our lives and sealed the deal. We bought him that day. We call him "Chance."

A few weeks later we were cruising through the local farm store when I came across a big chalkboard with handwritten notes on it. "Good grass hay $5.00/bale." "Goats for sale." "Laying hens." "Good horse, 15 years old, make offer."

Then one caught my eye. "Palomino mare, 9 years old, $800.00."

I love palominos and that was not a bad price. She was not too old, but not real young. I wondered if she was broke, had a good temperament, etc. I wrote the phone number down on a scrap of paper.

The owner had a large herd of horses and was trying to downsize. We arrived at his ranch to see a beautiful palomino alone in a round pen. Her name was Lakota. She seemed edgy and uneasy with us. She had been ridden before, but the owner didn't want the liability of letting us ride her on his property. No red flag there!

"She hasn't been ridden in a while. She'll take some work," he explained.

We decided to buy her anyway and "work with her." Besides, we liked her name too.

Our last equine acquisition was a surprise. Nissa started equine therapy with a type of horse called "fox trotters." This particular breed of horse has a gait similar to how humans walk. Riding these horses is thought to help neuro-reprogramming with brain injuries.

Lakota had injured her leg and we were taking her to the vet the same morning that Nissa had a riding session scheduled. We offered to give her a ride since her riding stable and the vet were in the same neighborhood. That is how we ended up with the horse trailer at the ranch where this little pony lived.

Watching Nissa ride around the arena is not all that interesting after a couple of rounds, so her equine therapist sent us out back to look at her collection of equine friends.

"Do you want to take one home?" A voice called from behind us.

Tim and I answered immediately, in stereo, and with perfect timing calling out "no" as we turned to see who asked the question.

Nissa's riding teacher had left Nissa with an assistant and came out to join us.

"I'll give you that one for free," she said as she pointed at the little, brown, fuzzy pony standing at the edge of the herd.

"No thanks." We both smiled and agreed that we did not need another horse.

I'm not sure what happened but before the lesson was over, we were loading up little "Majestic" into the trailer. He was a scrawny little thing that looked picked on and certainly didn't match his name. He was very nervous when we got him home and jumped the same fence that kept the other two securely in. We wondered what we had gotten into.

It took a while for him to warm up to us, and a while for us to find a name that fit him. I eventually renamed him Chocolate Chip because he was so little and brown and sweet. We assumed he would stay pony size and hoped he would be a good horse for the girls. We were very surprised to see what happened through the winter as he got plenty to eat. He actually grew up to be a real horse so we shortened his name to Choco.

The horses each have a distinct personality and social order that fascinates me. Chance is very easy going and social, but not very directable. He is mellow to ride but goes where he wants to go, and doesn't pay much attention to what you want. He is curious and helpful. While building fence, he is good to pick up tools and carry them off somewhere in the field, likes to get into drinks, and generally has his nose between your hands to see what you are working on. He removes hats from heads and relocates coats left hanging on a fence post.

Lakota is high-strung, jumpy, and has clearly been traumatized by people. She wants to interact, but is always watching for danger. She often reacts to innocent movements as if they are a threat to her. She sometimes has dramatic reactions to sounds and novel situations. It takes a long time for her to settle down once you are in the saddle on her back. When she finally relaxes and settles into the ride, she is like a Ferrari. You even think "turn" and she is turning. She is very sensitive to your movement in the saddle, your instincts, and your emotion. And sometimes she seems to want to see how good a cowboy you really are!

Choco is playful, curious, and intuitive. He learns quickly and is eager to please. He enjoys interacting with people, but is also a tease. He has learned to jump and follow commands on the ground. He loves to run in the field and when he does, he glides in a beautifully smooth way. It almost looks like he is flying instead of running.

Horses have a social order of dominance that I am told has something to do with survival in the wild. In domesticated herds, there is a pecking order established; but I question if it would translate to survival if it came right down to it.

In our little herd, Lakota is the boss lady, alpha mare. She whinnies every morning as soon as she hears the back door open and continues her horse chatter until she has been fed. As we approach with a handful of hay for the first feeder, she turns and nips at anyone in the vicinity to let them know that the first is for her. If anyone is in kicking distance, they get a little kick too.

Once Lakota is munching happily on her first few bites, Chance starts nipping at Choco. Chance stands guard over the second feeder until it has some hay in it, gives Choco gestures to stay away, and then starts munching on his stash.

Once Choco gets to start eating in feeder number three, the dominance game goes to level two. Level two is where Lakota decides that someone has something better than her so she moves to one of the other feeders and chases off whomever is there, who chases off the next one, who goes to the first feeder and continues the meal.

I've tried messing with the social order just to see what happens. I'll feed them in a random order by starting with the second feeder or the third feeder. This causes temporary confusion but the boss lady quickly steps in and establishes that the first bite is hers. The two boys will fuss with each other a little and then settle back into the usual social order.

If this social order were functional for survival, it would suggest that the self-selected alpha mare would be the one to lead and protect the herd. The reality is that when there is potential for danger, she runs away in a panic, wildly kicking and bucking as if she is fighting for her life. This startles the other two, who watch her and look around trying to figure out what the big deal is. I really do not see her as a leader or as having good instincts in tense situations. In real danger, I think she would probably be of little help to the herd. She would be busy dealing with her own reactions.

Our second in the pecking order is Chance. When there is something new and potentially dangerous on the farm, he looks up from grazing, watches Lakota freak out, watches the novel situation, and then goes back to grazing. His lack of response suggests to me that he would be of little assistance to the herd either.

At the bottom of the hierarchy in our barn is Choco. He is the last to eat and the least concerned about getting his needs met. When there is perceived danger, he alerts the others and is very attentive to the circumstances, but non reactive. He carefully moves himself away from the stimulus, where he remains attentive at a safe distance. He is agile, fast, and very instinctive. He is social with the horses in the next pasture. In a real crisis, I think he would be the one who would survive and lead others to safety.

People seem to establish similar social structures for probably the same primitive reasons. I think people have it mixed up now too. There are those who are loud, demanding, and see that their needs are met first. Having those needs met benefits them, but not the herd as a whole. They get what they think they need because they squawk and fight for it even if it means hurting others.

Nissa is at the other end of the spectrum and reminds me of Choco. She does not demand that her needs be met, but has a calm assurance that they will be. She is instinctive and saves her energy for the situations that require action. She lets others push ahead of her, get there first, and get more than her, and yet she manages to get enough for her needs. She is smart in a quiet, non-intrusive way, but can kick it up a notch if she needs to.

A plaque hangs on her wall that reads, "Thou art the potter, I am the clay." She continues to move forward with the belief that all will be well and that she will benefit from all of her life experience. Saint Mark of the New Testament said, "But many that are first shall be last; and the last shall be first." I suspect that she is planting seeds that will reap a rich harvest for her somewhere in the future. In the meantime, I think she is becoming bulletproof thanks to some of her life challenges.

CHAPTER 22

Hawaii

Early on during the rehabilitation hospital stay, progress was slow; what looked like depression started to set it. There were frequent episodes of tears and a noticeably lower energy level. Depression is common in stroke survivors and other brain injuries, so this development was not a surprise to the treatment team.

The doctor started her on an anti-depressant and I started her on an internal refocus campaign. I thought it might help if she had something to think about and look forward to. She needed something to offset the tedious day-to-day grind of trying to do things that her body wasn't able to do.

"Try to move your tongue, try to move your hand, try to close your fingers, try to make this sound, try to stand a little longer, try to hold your head straight, try, try, try ..." Her therapists were remarkable people - determined, positive, and caring; but recovery was slow and discouraging. The art of celebrating an inch, when you still have a mile to go, was what rehab was all about. It would have been easy to just resign to being paralyzed and sink into self pity.

"Nissa, think of somewhere you have always wanted to go - anywhere, anywhere at all." Her eyes looked at me with a blankness that told me she was not engaged.

"Is there someplace you dreamed of going someday?" I really

wanted to coax an answer from her.

I watched her eyes closely, but all I saw was the same blank stare.

"There must be someplace you've wanted to go on vacation." I persisted.

She eventually blinked at me.

"Have you thought of someplace?"

She blinked.

"Spell it for me," I said and then started our alphabet routine.

"A, B, C, D, E, F, G, H"

She blinked.

"It starts with H?" I asked to clarify.

She blinked, so I wrote an "H" on the little dry erase board that we used when we talked.

"A," I started again when she blinked right away.

I wrote an "A" next to the "H."

"Hawaii?" I guessed.

Her eyes lightened just a little as she blinked.

I smiled back. "You'd like to go to Hawaii on vacation?"

She blinked.

"Tell you what. You get yourself out of this bed and I'll take you to Hawaii. Do we have a deal?"

She blinked but I couldn't read her reaction, so I didn't know if it would help motivate her or not.

The next day I arrived at her room with lots of aloha supplies. I found a Hawaiian calendar with big colorful pictures on it. I tore the pictures off the calendar and taped them all over her room. I bought a Hawaiian print shirt and hung it so it swung just below the television right in front of her bed. I hung plastic flower leis around the room and put a coconut shell sculpture on her bedside tray. I thought it would at least make the room a little more cheery.

It was now 2005, three years later. She had been living with me for a year and a half and the reality of losing her home, her marriage, and her children was settling in. Everything she had lived for was slipping away. Her life would not be what she had pictured, dreamed of, and worked for. Her grief was regularly salted with doses of conflict and hostility from "the other party."

"The other party" was the legal term for the other Smith in the "Smith vs. Smith" cases brought before the judge for resolution. They were still not divorced and custody of the children was not final. He had moved himself and the children into his girlfriend's house and attempted to restrict Nissa's contact with the children.

It took a special court order to allow the children to have predictable phone contact with their mother. The State code outlines minimum visitation guidelines for non-custodial parents, but suggests that contact beyond the minimal outlined should be encouraged. In the "Smith vs. Smith" case, any more than the outlined minimal visitation had to be ordered by the court before the "other party" would agree to it. It was an ugly and sad time for her.

From the outside, it appeared as if another refocus was in order. The journey was getting really tough again. This time it was emotionally tough rather than physically tough. I was afraid that she was a prime target for another depression to hit. I hoped we could ward it off with a good distraction.

"Nissa, do you remember when I decorated your hospital room with all that Hawaiian stuff?"

"Nyeah." Her affirmative answer was very nasal and I often had difficulty understanding if she was saying "na" or "yeah." This time it didn't matter because I was going to go on, whether she remembered or not.

"I told you that if you got out of that hospital bed that I would take you to Hawaii."

She looked at me intently.

"Well, I have never made good on that promise. What would you think about going to Hawaii?"

"OK," she answered before it had really sunk in.

"I've been thinking about it," I continued. "We could leave Thursday morning after your mid-week visit with the kids and come home on Tuesday night so we'll be back for your next mid-week visit. We'll go on a weekend the kids are not here. Maybe we could get Mom to go too and one of us can man the luggage and one of us can man the wheelchair. What do you think?"

This time the "okay" had a little more energy behind it.

Mom agreed to go, Tim donated the frequent flyer miles, and I started searching for a condo to stay in. Every day after work and chores, I got online and then shared my findings with Nissa. We talked about options and plans, and then locked in dates, tickets, and lodging.

This would be Nissa's first trip anywhere since the stroke. She had not been in a car for more than a couple of hours, so a long airplane ride may prove challenging. I was a little nervous about being the tour guide and chauffeur, and a little nervous about managing such a big trip with the disability factor for the first time. I wasn't sure what surprises we may run into.

The three of us piled all of our things into one large and one small suitcase so that one person could manage that department. We opted to keep her wheelchair with us so we could use it on the layover in Los Angeles and as soon as we got off the plane in Hawaii. We hoped that it would be safer with us than going through as a piece of luggage.

The flight over went well. I managed to find our condo on the other side of the island without getting lost. We quickly settled in for a few days of sightseeing and relaxation.

We discovered that wheelchairs and soft sandy beaches were not a good mix. Nissa wears a brace on her left leg to help stabilize her ankle. Without the brace she is fairly wobbly. Without the brace on the sand she was really wobbly, but we did the beach anyway. She also learned how quickly skin burns on areas where there is poor circulation. Other than that, the trip was great. Nissa fatigued easily but wanted to go and see and experience everything that she could.

The week flew by. On the way home I asked, "What did you think of Hawaii?"

She replied, "It was surreal. I didn't really get to soak it in. I need to go again sometime."

I just smiled and said "okay."

CHAPTER 23

First Day of School

I stare at a picture from before the stroke. Long, dark hair drapes over her shoulders, framing a face with character and definition. A quiet dignity emanates from her aura. I look harder at the picture trying to remember who she was before this life-altering event turned her inside out.

She used to be a working mother, holding down a full-time job, and caring for her two young daughters. She hoped to quit work after the third child was born to be a stay-at-home mom.

She had always been quiet, never much to say and intensely private. She liked to laugh. She liked crafts, but also liked being out of doors. She was more of a follower than a leader, but also very independent.

This particular day I am dropping her off for her first day of college, post stroke. She had a two-year degree from her pre-stroke life, but could no longer use any of those skills. She was headed back to school, mostly to have something to do during the day.

I parked in a handicapped space in front of the building where we had gone for her admission interview. The interviewer was visibly uncomfortable with my presence. I gave her a brief introduction of Nissa and told her that I would be there to help interpret if she couldn't understand what Nissa was saying.

Some people caught on to her distorted speech and were patient with sorting out what she was saying. Others became easily discouraged and welcomed the interpretation. The explanation relaxed the interviewer some, but she still seemed uncomfortable. I got the impression that she did not want someone watching her interviewing skills and she felt like it was demeaning to Nissa.

I decided to let Nissa make the decision since it was her interview.

"Nissa, do you want me to wait outside?" I asked sincerely. I really wanted to know if she wanted to go it alone.

Nissa shook her head "no."

The interviewer silently conceded to my presence. She also asked as many "yes" and "no" questions as she could so that language was not a barrier. The two of them did just fine without me. It was always a dilemma for me to know when I would be helpful and when I would be a hindrance. It was always an adventure to work through the various reactions people had to Nissa's disability and what it would take to accommodate for it.

It had started to rain lightly. I ducked my head as I got out of the car to unload her wheelchair. As I wheeled the chair around to her door, I noticed that the walkway leading to the front of the building had an uphill slope.

Nissa was able to paddle the ground with her right leg and push the wheel on the chair with her right hand. If she was on flat ground, she was able to get around for short distances without going in circles. I didn't know if she could make it up an incline like this one.

I steadied the chair while she plopped into it.

"Got your back pack?" I asked.

"Yeah."

"Ready to conquer the academic world?" I teased.

She just laughed.

I wheeled her around, pointed the wheelchair toward the door, and gave it a strong push to get her headed up the sloping side walk.

"Good luck today," I yelled as the rain began to fall a little harder.

I shut her car door and then headed to the back of my SUV to shut the cargo door where the wheelchair had been stored. By then I was getting pretty wet, so I ran to my door and jumped in the car.

I immediately looked over to see how Nissa was doing. Her head was down to shield her face from the now drizzling rain. She was struggling one inch at a time to make it up the slope. She stopped and put her one good hand above her eyes as she looked out to see how much further she had to go. Letting go of the wheelchair wheel caused her to start rolling backwards. She attempted to brake with her one good foot.

My heart immediately moved to rescue mode and I wanted to leap out of the car to save her. But I stopped myself.

"She can do this on her own. Let her go." I started a conversation in my head to try to soothe what my heart was feeling. I put my head down on the steering wheel so that I would quit watching her struggle. I said a little prayer that she would be okay today and others would be courteous and know when to offer help. Little things like getting in and out of bathrooms with double doors and narrow halls can be close to impossible alone, in a wheelchair, with only one good hand.

When I looked up again she was close to the front doors. I let out a sigh of relief and felt a little silly for being so worried about her.

Her next obstacle was the heavy set of entry doors that she was squarely in front of. They too could be difficult to maneuver from a wheelchair. At least she was out of the rain.

I looked down to turn the key and start the engine of my car. When I looked back up a man had approached Nissa and was talking to her. He opened the door for her and waited for her to paddle through it and then opened the next door too.

I felt foolish as my eyes filled with tears, but I was deeply grateful that someone had come along to help her. It reassured me that she would be okay and that others would be there when I could not.

I chastised myself a little for the emotion. "She's a grown woman. She's been to college before. She's not helpless. You don't have to hover over her. You probably drive her crazy sometimes with your mothering."

That is what I felt like. I was the Mom sending my kindergartener off to her first day of school. I wanted her to fit in. I wanted others to be nice to her. I wanted her to succeed. I wanted her to like school. I wanted her to be able to figure everything out.

The stroke started her over in life. Not only did she have to learn to use her body again, she had to learn to interact all over again. She had a vulnerable aura about her that usually struck a chord in anyone who tuned in. Her vulnerability often elicited kindness in others. Once in a while, it elicited a predatory response. I wasn't sure she would recognize when she was prey. She was vulnerable and easy bait for a wolf in sheep's clothing.

"What could go wrong at school?" I asked myself as I drove away. Probably the worst thing would be that she would get stuck in the bathroom and not be able to get the door open and her wheelchair through it. Or she would try to take notes but not be able to keep up. Her fine motor skills were returning, but took a great deal of concentration.

"Oh, she'll be okay," I told myself and then decided not to think about it anymore.

I called mid day to make sure the Paratransit found her to take her home. We had been told that they would not drop her off for some reason. Then we were told they would drop her off, but not at that building. Then we were told they would drop her off and pick her up, but they weren't used to going to that building. I thought there was a 50/50 chance the ride home would get messed up and then I would have to use my lunch hour to take her home.

As it turned out, the day went "fine." "Fine" was Nissa's word for okay and her answer to most of my questions about how things are. I've never been able to understand what "fine" really means to her, but she says it a lot. Maybe it's just easy to say, and non-committal, so that she does not have to try to explain how things really are. Communicating is a lot of work still and she is often misunderstood.

The class she took was only once a week, but lasted all morning. I dropped her off in the morning on my way to work and she took the bus home in the afternoon. School was "okay" but didn't "fill" her life like we hoped it would. Her eyes were still not able to focus, so reading and typing was a real challenge and took a long time. She was difficult to understand, so she couldn't really interact with anyone. She couldn't take notes because she couldn't write fast enough to record anything. Mobility was difficult even with the wheelchair, and her electric scooter was not allowed on the Paratransit bus (it was half an inch too long for their standards).

It helped us to realize the challenges she would face if she ever tried to go back to work. She had residual visual, fine motor, communication, and mobility challenges, and was very slow with anything she did. I couldn't think of any employment situation that could accommodate for that many disabilities and still be profitable for an employer.

Nissa's real goal was to be a full-time mother. She is a creative cook and manages put together some fun meals for the kids. Carli calls them "Mama's esperiments." Nissa also keeps our dishwasher loaded and unloaded, and stays on top of the laundry. She is immensely patient and spends hours reading, playing board games, and listening to the girls as they share their life adventures with her. She managed to recover all of the emotional and physical skills necessary to parent her children.

My life has moments of pure serenity as I watch the four of them together. Nissa's purpose in life right now is clearly centered in her girls. She is very intuitive about their needs. The children respond to her touch, her voice, her presence in their lives, and her homemade cookies.

Cowgirls

CHAPTER 24

Can We Have a Horse Show?

Horse Show weekend was magical. The girls were totally in a childhood "zone" where they successfully brought a fantasy into reality. They were imaginative, dedicated, creative, and powerful. Each did what only they could do, and at the same time worked together to bring about a collective vision. They reminded me of what was possible when you believe.

"Can we have a horse show?" McKenzie must have been appointed to be the spokesperson.

"Sure," I answered without much thought as to what that really meant. I wasn't sure why there was a hint of glee in their young eyes as I delivered my answer.

The next thing I knew, a piece of poster board purchased for another project was on the kitchen counter with the words "Horse Show" printed boldly across the top. I couldn't say anything; after all, I had been the one to give permission for the event.

"What time should we do the show?" the eager voice asked.

We briefly discussed the best time of day for the show. Grandma and Grandpa were scheduled to arrive in the early afternoon, so later in the afternoon would accommodate a larger audience for the show.

The rest of the poster quickly took form with the date, time, place, and a youthful plea for attendees. McKenzie was pleased with the poster, and searched for an appropriate location in the house to display it.

A while later as I lugged a basket of dirty clothes into the laundry room, the formerly clean counter top caught my eye. It was cluttered with cardboard toilet paper roll ends, paint, and painting supplies.

"Where did you get all of those toilet paper things?" I asked in a voice laced with a touch of repulsion.

"I've been saving them," the young triumphant voice answered.

"Where have you been saving them?" I asked even though I wasn't sure I wanted to know.

"Under my bed," she offered, a little more hesitant.

"How long have you been saving them?" I was really wondering if there were piles of unrolled toilet paper somewhere in my house or yard or barn or ditch or office.

"I've been saving them for a long time," she proudly answered.

"Why have you been saving toilet paper rolls?" I asked.

"I wanted to make something out of them," she replied very confidently.

"I see you have decided to make something out of them today." My voice was more neutral now.

Her eyes brightened as she eagerly shared her plan. "I have nine of them."

She then lined three of them up, one behind the other in a row. "These three I'm going to paint blue. They will be the first place trophies."

She then lined up three more. "I'm going to paint these red. They are going to be the second place trophies."

"I'm just going to leave the last piece of toilet paper on these three because it's white. They will be the third place trophies." She lined them up in a neat row too.

"Where did you get the paint?" I was curious about how she found things in the house that I didn't even know we had around.

"They're Mom's," she quickly answered.

"Does Mom know you are borrowing them?" I challenged.

At that point she strategically opened a bottle of paint and started decorating one of the trophies before she answered.

"She won't care," she replied with a hint of slyness in her voice.

By then I had the laundry loaded in the washer and was ready to continue with my Saturday chores. I didn't want to watch the laundry room being transformed to a paint shop. It would discourage me from attempting to clean any part of the house on a day when projects were underway.

I gathered up the sacks from inside all of the waste baskets in the house and headed to the back door to toss them in the garbage can outside. From the back porch I heard a young voice echoing from the barn with commanding tones. I decided to check out what was going on in the barn.

Shylee, the oldest girls, had the three horses all haltered and two of them tied to the hitching post. The third horse was being directed and commanded by the young equine enthusiast.

"What are you doing?" I asked curious about what she was up to.

"I'm training the horses for the horse show," she answered with a little irritation in her voice.

I guess I should have figured that out on my own.

"Oh," I responded as I watched her focus on the horse. It was starting to dawn on me that we were really going to have a horse show.

She had set up a series of jumps in the enclosed riding arena out back of the barn. She intended to put each of the three horses on a lunge line and have them run around the arena and over the progressively-higher jumps. Maneuvering the jumps would be the basis for the show and what the horses would be judged on.

I was amazed at her intensity. She knew exactly what she wanted the horses to accomplish. Her vision and intention was easily transferred to the horses. The massive animals submitted to the "in charge" commands coming from her small frame. She was 100 percent immersed in her mission to get the horses ready for the show.

I watched long enough to satisfy myself that she would be safe with the horses. They tended to like kicking up their heels and nipping at each other when they were excited and getting attention, but she seemed to have them totally under control. I had never seen her work with the horses like this before, nor had I seen the horses respond like they were responding. I was impressed.

"Good job. Be careful," I called out as I went back to the house to continue my Saturday routine.

Entering the kitchen, I came across the next phase of horse show preparation. Carli, the youngest of the trio, had a big bowl out and had dumped a box of brownie mix into it. Nissa was helping her with the project.

"Are we having brownies for lunch?" I teased.

"No!" The answer came from a defiant little voice.

"Well, what are you doing?" I asked carefully so as not to stir up more aggravation.

"We're making treats to sell at the horse show," she answered in a determined voice.

"Oooh," I responded in a tone that communicated that I understood.

Just then, McKenzie popped into the kitchen with another sheet of poster board that had also been purchased for another purpose. She had already commissioned it for the horse show. There was a look of pride in her eyes as she flipped it around for us to see.

"Refreshments" was written boldly across the top of the poster.

"Brownies 5 cents, Lemonade 10 cents" was carefully printed further down the poster.

"You are going to sell treats at the horse show?" I asked surprised.

"Yep," came the confident reply!

"I need something to make lemonade with. What have we got?" Kenzie was a woman with a mission.

"Put it on the shopping list. We need to go to the store this afternoon anyway." I was now officially enrolled in the vision.

"Okay," she said, sounding relieved that I was not going to object to the plan.

But then how could I object when it was already on the poster? Kenzie was also a smart one with things like that.

I went back into the laundry room to rotate clothes from the washer to the dryer and then start another load in the washer. The counter top was splattered with paint. Three rows of brightly colored toilet paper roll trophies were drying amidst the splatters.

Further down the counter top, a pile of construction paper was spread around with certain colors selected and set up on the top of the pile. A little pair of scissors lay beside a sheet of blue paper. A picture of a blue ribbon, like the kind you would see at a county fair, had been laid on the blue construction paper and outlined.

About then, McKenzie bounced back into the laundry room and over to the construction paper project.

"Where did you get the picture of the ribbon you are tracing?"

"The internet," she volleyed, matter-of-factly.

"When did you get on the internet?"

"This morning," she answered quickly.

"My goodness, you have been busy!" I exclaimed.

"Yep," she answered with a big smile on her face.

I walked over to take a closer look at this project. She was going to trace and cut out blue, red, and white ribbons to go along with the trophies. She also had a sheet of yellow paper and was working on cutting out large stars.

"What are those?" I asked pointing to the stars.

"Those are the badges for the cops," she said intently.

"You're going to have security guards at the horse show?" I asked for clarity.

"No, I'm going to have cops there and these are their badges." She was clear about what she wanted at the show.

"Wow, looks like you've thought of everything!" My voice reflected respect.

"Yep," she answered as she continued working on her project.

When Grandma and Grandpa arrived they were presented with programs that doubled as invitations. Paper had been carefully folded in half with "Horse Show" printed on the outside. At the bottom, the date and time and place were neatly printed just like on the poster.

Inside the program, the horses were listed on the left-hand side with their owners listed on the right-hand side. The girls had agreed that each of them would own one of the horses. Below the horse's names, the events were listed. Walk, trot, and canter would be the events for the day.

The girls were restless at dinner that night. The horse show they had worked so hard on all day was to occur as soon as the dinner dishes were in the dishwasher.

The children ate quickly and then ran to the barn to get the horses ready and the show all set up. By the time the adults got dinner cleaned up and wandered out to the event arena, there was a table for the judge with all the trophies and ribbons lined up, spectator chairs awaiting guests, and horses haltered and tied up.

The horses had ribbons tied in their manes and brightly colored bailing twine braided in their tails. The girls were in their cowgirl boots and western shirts. The poster advertising the show leaned against the fence by the main arena gate. Refreshments were waiting in the house.

As the adults arrived at the arena, they were given assignments. "Mama" was assigned the first and most prestigious job.

"You get to be the judge, Mama!" one of the girls was excited to announce.

"You sit over here by the trophies," she said, while pointing to the table where the carefully arranged trophies and ribbons waited.

Nissa smiled and made her way to the judge's table. The horses were getting restless as the guests arrived, so Uncle Tim went to see if he could calm them. He was assigned to be the barn boy who helped with the horses. He dutifully accepted his assignment since that is what he planned to do anyway.

Grandma and Grandpa were given the best spectator seats. Aunt Teena, Jesse, and girlfriend all elected to stand so they could look over the fence panels instead of through them to view the show.

When I arrived, I was given one of the yellow stars and was told that I would be a cop, along with the dog, Brownie. I looked into the arena to see Brownie galloping around with a yellow star hooked to his collar.

As the show began, it was clear that some facilitation was

needed, so I stepped into the arena and declared myself the announcer. Projecting a Master of Ceremony, microphone kind of voice, I narrated the show and encouraged applause from the audience. Brownie galloped along side of the horses and barked encouragingly if they stalled at the jumps.

The wise judge saw that each horse and each owner received a first place trophy and ribbon for one of the three events.

The horse show was a great success. The girls were proud of their production and felt good about how their hard work had been received by the audience. The adults were impressed with what the little people had done and showered them with praise. The horses seemed to enjoy the new jumping skills they mastered and the dog loved herding the horses around the arena.

It is the kind of weekend that fills my life with joy. Nissa and the children add a very rich dimension to our lives and memories like these will long warm my heart.

Shylee, McKenzie and Carli with Chance

CHAPTER 25

I Had a Nightmare

The children have a mid-week visit with their mother where they spend the night. This arrangement was suggested by a custody expert to allow the children more time with their mother, something he stated they needed. It was a much better arrangement than the previous two-hour, mid-week visit that had been occurring.

The new arrangement required that I transport the children back to their other house the next morning before school. It was generally about a forty minute trip and gave us ample time to visit about lots of things. I enjoyed hearing about chasing boys on the playground at recess and the exciting events at preschool.

I was surprised to find that the grade school jumprope rhymes had not changed in the forty years since I had been their age. They were shocked sometimes when I knew the words and chanted along with them.

"Cinderella, dressed in yella, went outside to kiss a fella, made a mistake, kissed a snake, ended up with a belly ache. How many doctors did it take?"

Our morning trips across the valley became a time of connecting that I enjoyed. On this particular morning, the oldest child, Shylee, began our journey with, "I had a nightmare last night." She is typically guarded about her inner world, so I was surprised at her eagerness to share her dream. I tried not to sound too interested as I asked her about it so that it would not scare her into a retreat.

She was eager to talk about the dream, but her emotional tone was wistful. It didn't seem like it was really a nightmare but a dream that stirred something deep inside of her. "Nightmare" was probably the best word she could find to describe her experience.

"We lived in a house that was half our Dad's house and half our Mom's house." She went on to describe a scene where her subconscious had obviously tried to blend her separated worlds. She smiled as she described the best of both of her worlds that had been rolled into one location.

I smiled and nodded as she talked, but I found myself drifting back to memories when this issue unexpectedly surfaced at other times. It sometimes came through innocent questions that bubbled up and spilled out.

"When is Mommy coming home?"

"Why does Mama live with you Aunt Geri?"

"Why can't Mama come to our house? She still lives there too!"

"Why doesn't Papa want Mama to live with us anymore?"

"What's a divorce?"

"When are Mama and Papa going to get together?"

"Wouldn't it be fun if Papa moved next door? Then we could come over every day after school!"

Sensing the pain behind the questions was always tough for me. On the surface, they are happy, well-adjusted kids dealing just fine with the changes in their lives. Underneath, they are confused and torn between two worlds that they love but have to bounce between. My heart broke every week as I watched them struggle with the inevitable separation process when it was time to leave.

They run to the barn to see all of the animals, pet them, talk to them, feed them, and whatever else they can think to do to prolong the time with them. Then it is back to the house and up to their rooms to look around, hug the stuffed animals, and survey the unfinished activities. Then down to Mom's room where they love to hang out and spend evenings huddled together on her bed to watch TV.

The disconnecting ritual is sometimes repeated more than once before they can be convinced to actually get in the car to leave. Then there is the "I forgot something in the house" routine as we are loaded in the car attempting to leave.

In the early days, the ritual included tears, anger, refusal to get in the car, hiding, or excessive silliness. The ride across the valley was tense, with fighting and unpleasantness.

The connection ritual when they first arrive is also emotional. They run to the barn to say hello to the animals, then around the yard to see if anything has changed, then into the house and up to their rooms, and then to their Mom to say "hello" and connect with her. There is generally a transition period where they are unsettled and sometimes moody. After passing through the re-entry phase, they settle into life at Mom's house and are happy and engaged.

We have tried many strategies to make the transition easier, but the truth is that it is just plain difficult. As the years have passed, things have become routine but it is definitely still difficult for them to volley back and forth between homes and parents that they love. I sometimes overhear them creating make-believe worlds where they have resolved this dilemma.

I have concluded that the judge involved in the divorce and custody issues should put the children in charge. They are really very intuitive about their needs.

CHAPTER 26

The Way It's Supposed To Be

Ben blew into our lives like a gust of wind. He has a powerful, penetrating energy that is counter balanced by a vulnerability that scares me. He came to the house to interview Nissa for participation in a project he was putting together. He was straight forward but tender, patient, and accepting during his interview. When he couldn't understand what she said, he patiently worked with her, listening carefully as he learned to understand her speech.

Most people are nervous or impatient and don't want to be rude, so they quickly turn to me to translate what Nissa is saying. I generally go to every "first appointment" with her and explain the situation.

"She had a stroke. Her speech is sometimes difficult to understand. She understands you and her mind works just fine. It's okay to ask her to repeat herself. It sometimes helps to guess at what you think you heard and have her tell you if you've got it right. If you get stuck, I will be happy to help translate." I generally gave the spiel so quickly that people had to really listen to even understand me.

Women are generally more patient and persistent in communication efforts. Men usually listen to one sentence and then turn to me. Nissa has to concentrate and deliberately form every syllable of every word. She also has to wait for an exhale because she does not have control of her diaphragm muscles. If her exhale runs out before the sentence is complete then she has to wait for the next exhale to finish.

The pace of her speech is faster than her walk, but slower than the average person is accustomed to listening. Her walk and talk require those interacting with her to slow down, tune in, and take their time - all of which are challenging for the average American.

Ben was different. He wasn't in a hurry, didn't need to get anything done, and didn't have expectations. He was content with whatever outcome that emerged. His interactive style with Nissa was respectful and therapeutically kind. He was warm but not overly so.

When people first meet Nissa they generally have an emotional reaction to her condition. The initial reaction is that of sympathy or mild repulsion. I think it is hard for many to see people who are disabled. This is followed by overly kind remarks or discomfort with further interaction at all. It is evident that her disability is difficult to get past and presents a confusing dilemma when first meeting her.

Ben didn't seem to notice her disability and gently worked his way around it to connect with Nissa. As usual, Nissa didn't have much to say, but the two of them had a simple chat at the kitchen counter while I fixed myself something to eat.

One of the questions Ben asked Nissa was, "If you could change something in your past, would you?"

She was quick to answer, "Yes."

"What would you change?" Ben cautiously questioned, knowing that he may be treading on ground too personal to share at a first encounter.

"This." She used her good hand to point out the paralysis on her left side.

"Oh," Ben said as he nodded his head and looked down at the paper where he was recording her answers.

"Really?" I butted into their interview.

She looked directly at me and with widened eyes and an animated tone, answered "yes."

I retracted myself from the interview and the evening ended uneventfully. I wondered what Ben would do with the information gained in his interview and what would become of his project. Nissa didn't seem to have any particular reaction to the evening, but she is hard to read. Her face doesn't have much muscle tone, and she is generally fairly flat in her emotions.

I concluded that it was a good evening because Ben had such a healthy approach to Nissa. It was fun for me to see someone take an interest in her for no apparent reason. Her social world is small and any addition to it is welcomed.

Several days later, I was in Nissa's bedroom gathering up dishes left there by the children who love to take food into her room and eat while they sit on her bed and watch "Animal Planet" on television.

I gave Nissa my California King-sized bed for her bedroom so all four of them would fit on it. There is plenty of room for sitting on it cross-legged to watch TV or play games.

They are all short enough to fit on it laying across it the shorter direction rather than lengthwise like you would normally lay in bed. The girls often preferred to all sleep with their Mom even though they have their own beds in their bedrooms. By morning it looks like a nest with legs and arms every which direction and blankets twisted over, under, and around the various sizes and shapes of bodies. It looks uncomfortable to me, but I think it's one of the few ways they have to compensate for all the time they do not have with their mother. They seem almost whole when they are snuggled under the blankets together.

Whenever my cupboards are looking a little bare I sweep through Nissa's part of the house and follow the trail of cups, plates, and bowls that usually start in the bedroom and end in the computer room. It represents the bedtime snacks and between-meals munchies that have wandered out of the kitchen. Nissa's one good hand is on her walking cane, so she can't carry the dishes back to the kitchen. The best she can do is to stack them up so they are ready to be transported. The girls are usually focused on trying to find their shoes and socks when it is time to leave, so the dishes often are forgotten.

I generally sweep through her part of the house a couple of times a week to gather dishes, empty waste baskets, and move laundry to and from the laundry room. Luckily Nissa can care for her own personal needs like showering and dressing, so she requires very little assistance. I was on one of my sweeps through her room when she stopped me.

"You know that question Ben asked me the other day?"

I was puzzled. I had not thought about the Ben encounter since it happened and wasn't sure what she was referring to. It took some back and forth questions and nods for me to get on the same page.

"Do you mean when he asked you if you could change something from your past?"

She answered with an affirmative nod.

I was intrigued. It was the question I had challenged her on and she had emphatically answered. I put down the dishes that I had collected, walked over to her bed, and sat down next to her.

She spoke a few words that I didn't understand because her emotion was already taking over. She attempted several times to speak, but each time the tears were stronger than her ability to deliver words.

I placed my hand on her back and breathed slowly, hoping that I could calm her with my energy. After a few minutes she was able to utter a simple phrase.

"This is the way it's supposed to be."

I wasn't sure I understood so I repeated the phrase.

"This is the way it is supposed to be?"

She nodded a "Yes."

"You mean what happened, happened for a reason? Like it has some purpose in the big picture of your life? It's not just an accident?" I questioned.

She nodded "Yes" and said, "It is supposed to be this way."

She had obviously wrestled with the issue. I'm sure it was not the first time she had wrestled with the question "Why?" or "Why me?" The answer to "Why?" was not evident, but she seemed to be at peace with the idea that she was not a victim of unfortunate circumstances.

Her tears were not tears of pain so much as an expression of deep understanding. The kind of "ah ha" experience that changes the way you see things. There was an air of acceptance in the emotion that passed through her that day.

When the tears had cleansed her passage, a peaceful feeling descended on her, soothing any remaining pain. I let the moment linger before introducing the journey again.

"So that doesn't mean you're done recovering, right?" My question was not worded well and confused her.

Her bowed head lifted up so her eyes could meet mine. There was a hint of bewilderment in them.

"You're still going to get better aren't you?" I delivered the question with a smile and hint of teasing.

"Yeah," she said with a big smile. "I'm still going to get better."

"Good," I declared as I got up to finish my dish gathering mission. "We've got a ways to go."

I left her sitting on the edge of her bed knowing that when she was ready, she would rejoin me on the path to wherever it is that we are going.

CHAPTER 27

Hyperbaric Treatment

The downside of scuba diving is coming back up to the surface. If a diver has been deep enough for long enough, they must carefully calculate their ascent or they could end up in serious trouble. Oxygen in the blood stream compresses as a diver descends. If the diver shoots to the surface too quickly, the oxygen will not have a chance to equalize and will expand after the diver has surfaced. This produces a very painful and possibly fatal condition known as the "Bends."

Hyperbaric chambers were invented to alleviate the Bends. The unfortunate diver would be rushed to an air-tight glass tube where the air would be compressed, simulating an ocean dive, and then slowly decompressed, simulating a slow return to the surface allowing the oxygen to equalize more normally in the blood stream.

I don't remember how we were first introduced to hyperbaric oxygen treatment for medical conditions, but it happened when Nissa first came to live with me. At the time, it was mostly in an experimental stage and had little evidential support. We heard some anecdotal information that was hopeful, and a theory that was plausible, but nothing solid that said it was a good idea.

It was seen by some as preying on unfortunate souls, desperate for hope, in hopeless situations. People will try anything when they have nothing to lose. It didn't sound like there was any risk of harm and maybe it would help. I figured we were one of those cases that had nothing to lose. I explained it all to Nissa. She was interested, so I took her to Salt Lake City for an intake at the hyperbaric facility.

Hopefully, the effect of hyperbaric treatment would be hyper oxygenation. Hyperbaric treatment dissolves extra oxygen into the blood plasma. Breathing pure oxygen at three-times the normal pressure delivers fifteen times as much physically dissolved oxygen to tissues as breathing room air. This promotes formation of new capillaries into wound areas and sufficient oxygen to meet the needs of oxygen-deprived areas. The extra oxygen concentration sometimes leads to additional recovery that may not otherwise have happened or happened much slower.

Some of Nissa's brain cells were obviously damaged by the stroke and would not recover. However, cells adjacent to the dead cells may still have some life but be undernourished because of their connection to the dead cells. If the undernourished cells could be revived by receiving oxygen, then her brain may be able to create new pathways to communicate with the rest of her body.

Our first trial was in the fall of 2003, almost two years after the stroke. The hyperbaric chamber was about forty-five minutes away by car and three hours away by public transportation. Nissa needed to attend daily for as long as possible. Finances would only allow a two-week trial, and public transportation was the only thing we could work out.

The two weeks were more of an adventure than we bargained for. I would bring Nissa into the city with me each morning and drop her off at a downtown bus stop. The bus driver sometimes noticed her sitting on the bench and waited for her to make her way to the door before zooming off to the next bus stop, and sometimes she was not noticed and got left. Nissa moved very slowly so it was probably difficult to determine if she intended to get on the bus.

If she made it on, she rode the bus to the first transfer point. On the days she got left at the first stop, I would make frantic phone calls to notify the Paratransit service that she had been left so that they would not penalize her if she missed their connection. I would then dash to the bus stop and rush her on to the transfer point hoping to get there for the next connection. I only got one speeding ticket and choose not to remember how many mad dashes from work I did during that time period.

At the first transfer station, she would switch from a bus to a light-rail system. This required her to navigate steps and distances that were treacherous for her. We discussed sending her by wheelchair rather than having her go on foot, but the wheelchair presented obstacles she could not maneuver alone. She had some interesting adventures and one marriage proposal at the public transfer station.

If she made it successfully to the light rail destination on time, she would travel by train to a stop where a Paratransit bus would pick her up and take her to the hyperbaric facility. If something went wrong and she got there late, the Paratransit bus would leave her and she would incur a demerit in their system. If she incurred three demerits she would not be allowed to use the Paratransit service for a prescribed period of time. So, one messed-up connection early in the day could mess up the connections for the rest of the day, resulting in her not being able to use the Paratransit service.

Once she arrived at the hyperbaric facility she had to change clothes. She had to be in perfectly clean, cotton clothes and be free of hairspray, hair gel, perfume, make-up, fingernail polish, or anything else that might ignite in an oxygen-rich environment. She had half an hour after arrival to change and enter the chamber.

The chamber consisted of a large glass cylinder positioned horizontally, about waist high off the ground. Nissa would lay on a gurney that slid into the glass tube. The tube was sealed by a door that looked like a submarine hatch door. The tube was clear so the patient could be visually monitored. The staff fondly referred to the treatment as a dive. The tube was also transparent, to reduce the probability of the patient experiencing a claustrophobic panic.

The chamber was equipped with the ability to communicate so that vocal monitoring could also take place. A television screen outside the chamber was positioned for movie or television watching. Nissa saw the first hour of many movies during her two week tenure.

I guess day-time television was not all that interesting to her.

The dive or treatment started with a slow compression of the air inside the chamber. Nissa would have to yawn or plug her nose and blow to equalize the air in her head much like when you are in an airplane or changing elevation while on a road trip in a car.

The staff would ask her every few minutes if she was doing okay. Having sinus problems or a cold could prevent the ability to successfully dive. There were a few days when I gave her a decongestant before she went just to make sure she wouldn't have problems. When she reached the compression level that equated to 30 feet under water, she would stay there for about 45 minutes before starting the slow decompression process. She would go through the same ear clearing ritual on the way up. Nissa was fortunate in that she never became claustrophobic and had no side effects or unusual reactions to the treatment.

Once out of the chamber, she had only 20 minutes to dress and get outside to wait for the Paratransit to pick her back up. You are required to be at your pick up location 10 minutes early in case the bus comes early and wait for it at least 20 minutes after the pick up time before you are allowed to call to see if you have been left or forgotten. The bus is supposed to wait for you for at least 5 minutes before leaving you. Sometimes the bus was on the opposite side of the building from where Nissa was waiting and it took Nissa too long to get to the bus. If the driver didn't notice the handicapped person walking their way, Nissa would get left even though she was at the right place, at the right time.

If Nissa made the Paratransit connection it would take her back to the light rail station. She would then do the treacherous transfer to the bus. If those connections were all on time, then she would be waiting at the bus stop at 5:00 p.m. and I would pick her up on my way home from work. It was an all-day event to accomplish a one-hour treatment.

We packed a sack lunch every day that she would eat somewhere along the way. She didn't dare drink anything all day because she didn't have time or access to a restroom, except occasionally at the hyperbaric facility if everything was on schedule.

The two-week ordeal was a taxing episode we were glad see come to an end. It demonstrated incredible independence and courage on Nissa's part, but was very tiring. It was nerve racking, worrisome, and disruptive for me, but also felt like a victory. We were exhausted and relieved enough when it was over that it took a while to ask the question, "Did it do any good?"

I began to watch her as I held the question in my mind. I thought I saw changes that were gradual and subtle, but wasn't sure. It may have just been my desire to see a difference rather than any real change. Or maybe I was watching so closely that I was just seeing some things for the first time because I simply hadn't paid attention to them before.

Eventually I started asking, "Did you fall today?" The answer again and again was "no." Nissa used to fall at least once a day, more days than not. I thought I saw her walking more naturally and with better balance. The not falling was evidence that what I thought I saw may actually be true.

The episodes of falling eventually subsided, except for occasions when she tried to walk, talk, and chew gum at the same time. Sometimes she would go into autopilot when she was walking where she stopped commanding every step. Autopilot mode sometimes resulted in a fall as well. She still had to watch her feet and control every step with a conscious signal from her brain. She couldn't look up or talk or even think about anything else. So once in a while there was still a spill to the ground, but for the most part the days of broken ribs, broken ankles, bumps, and bruises had come to an end.

The other area that slowly improved was her speech. She was easier to understand and seemed to have better control of her breath. She was able to talk without waiting for an exhale, and was able to enunciate letters rather than just making general sounds. Communication became clearer in the month that followed the first round of hyperbaric treatment.

It was some time after the first hyperbaric experiment that the divorce papers arrived and all of her emotional and financial resources went to the legal battles that ensued for the next few years.

I told Nissa that I thought that hyperbaric treatment had helped and that another trial some day may be worth it. We wondered from time to time if and when "someday" would arrive.

In the mean time, the medical community pursued the use of hyperbaric treatment for a variety of medical conditions and made some head way with legitimizing it. It quickly became recognized as a justifiable treatment for carbon monoxide poisoning, acute cyanide poisoning, burns, crush injuries, interstitial bleeding, anemia, ischemia (lack of blood supply to an organ or tissue), and maybe in acute brain and spinal injuries.

One day I saw a newspaper article that the local hospital was installing a large hyperbaric chamber. It was so big that multiple patients could walk in and be seated for their compression voyage. In the newspaper picture, it looked like a little submarine. The inside was equipped with upright seats and audio/visual entertainment. It was definitely high tech and medically sanctioned. Insurance would even pay for treatment of some diagnoses.

I go to the hospital every week as part of my work routine. One day as I was walking down the hall, I felt impressed to take a side trip to the hyperbaric area. I hadn't thought about hyperbarics for a long time, so the impression that came that day surprised me. I made my way to the waiting area and approached the counter where the glass windows were closed.

As I stepped up to the counter, someone leaned forward to slide the glass window open. The lean forward motion drew my attention to a set of large bosoms that looked like they were about to fall out of the low-necked, skin-tight, shirt that was struggling to hold them in. That was not what I expected to see at a medical facility. I took a deep breath and shifted my eyes from her chest up to her face.

The next thing that caught my attention was a jaw chomping wildly on a wad of gun. I looked around behind me to make sure I hadn't stepped into the local diner instead of a medical waiting room. There was one man sitting there with a silly expression on his face and a far-away look in his eyes. I figured he had just been treated to the lean-forward show and was basking in the after glow.

I turned back around, determined to actually make eye contact with the woman. She looked to be about nineteen years old. She stared at me like she wasn't sure if she was going to help me or not. Of course, it did take me a minute to get around to saying something so maybe she thought I had a compromised brain and was there for some oxygen.

I did finally compose myself enough to say that I had some questions about hyperbaric treatment.

"What d'ya wanna know?" she asked matter of fact like between chomps of her gum.

"Umm, do you need a doctor's referral? Do you need to be under a doctor's care? What kind of conditions do you treat? Does insurance cover it? Things like that." I tried to paint a general picture of what I needed to know.

"Ja' wanna talk to the doctor?" she offered through the chomps.

"Do you mean I could talk to the hyperbaric doctor right now?" That one took me more off guard than the bosom encounter.

"Yeah, if he's here. J'wanna talk to 'im?" she offered.

"Yes, that would be great if I could talk to him." I couldn't imagine it would actually happen; but my encounter up to that point had been interesting, so I decided to be hopeful as she disappeared around the corner.

She reappeared a few minutes later and announced: "Yeah, he'll talk to ya, but he only has a few minutes."

"Come on, I'll letcha in." She nodded for me to go to the door.

I think the walk and talk with the doc helped dispel some of her built-up energy because the gum chomping slowed down and nearly came to a stop by the time she delivered me to the doctor's private office.

From her warning, "he only has a few minutes," I expected a hurried conversation with someone who felt obligated to go through the motions of a quasi consultation. While I was thrilled to have gotten past the locked door, my expectations were guarded.

I don't remember his name, but he had a warm and gentle handshake. His respectful attitude and the professional consultation delivered with softness and sincerity were unforgettable- yet another surprise that caught me off guard.

Being mindful of his time, I rattled off a brief description of Nissa's condition and my list of questions as quickly as I could. I could see by his face that he had a less-than-positive response, but would deliver it gently.

"There is no evidence to suggest that hyperbaric treatment will help your sister. The progress you saw before may have just been part of her natural recovery. Our treatments here last for two hours at a time and cost $2,500.00 per treatment. It is simply not reasonable to spend that kind of money on a treatment that has no evidence to back it, and her insurance will not pay for it. I'm sorry."

He was brave enough to maintain eye contact during and after the delivery of his bad news. I was quiet, but held a determined look in my eyes while I formulated a response. I think he could see that I wasn't going to give up that easily, so interrupted me before I even got started with round two.

"There is a research project underway at LDS hospital in Salt Lake City. I'm pretty sure they are still looking for subjects. They are trying to determine if hyperbaric treatment is effective with recovery from anoxic brain injuries. The treatment is free, but there are some requirements that may be difficult."

He retrieved a business card from a stack on his desk and wrote down a name and phone number.

"You may want to call them and see what you think of the research project. I'm sorry we can't help you here. Good luck with your sister."

"Thank you," I offered with a genuine feeling of gratitude. I was grateful for his humanness and for the information, but was thrown by the turn in the road. I hadn't expected to be directed to another hospital. I was hoping for the convenience of the local hospital. We had paid $100.00 per treatment before, so to hear that the treatments were $2,500.00 nearly choked me. Free treatment with a few strings attached maybe wasn't so bad.

The connection I eventually made at the hospital was with a nurse named Sue. She ran the research project. She was cheerful but direct. I liked her immediately. We discussed some basics about

Nissa's condition and history. Sue determined that Nissa met the basic criteria for the research project. The next step was to meet in person for some additional preliminary checks before being formally accepted for the study.

Nissa would be given 60 treatments delivered on consecutive days except for weekends. That meant Monday through Friday, every day for 3 months. She would need to travel to the next county every day. The trip would take 65 minutes one way, by car, on a good traffic day. An hour treatment, time needed to park, get to the hyperbaric area of the hospital, change, and then change again and get back to the car for the 65-minute ride home. That would add up to three and half to four hours each day. With the Paratransit, it would be another all-day event if even possible at all.

The crucial question that everything hinged on was eventually asked.

"How will she get here?" Sue was concerned because of the distance we would need to travel.

"Well, we're exploring options," I offered carefully.

Sue had hopeful reactions to some of the options. When I mentioned the Paratransit service it brought an immediate reaction.

"Oh God, don't do that to her. She'd have to just spend the night here sometimes." She mentioned something about the worry it would cause her. I knew it would cause me worry too. Nissa's limitations and the Paratransit's limitations were not a good match. When I discussed the situation with the Paratransit service, they also were skeptical about being able to pull it off reliably.

Sue wanted us to work the transportation issue out, but cautioned that the research project was not worth any permanent trauma. We struggled for weeks with this option or that, trying to find something that was feasible and workable and that could be sustained for 3 months. When we finally settled on a plan, we reviewed it with Sue who hesitantly agreed. She was appropriately skeptical and offered an out.

"If you have to drop out of the study for some reason, we can negotiate returning some of the fee."

There was a fee for participating in the research project. The fee was to recover a small portion of the cost and to ensure a level of commitment from participants. It was paid up front to also ensure participation to completion.

So here was the plan: We hired a college-aged young woman to drive 3 days a week. On the days she could not drive, we would search for family and friends to fill in. The other two days a week would be manned by volunteer drivers from our church.

The trip would begin after kids were in school and the morning rush hour on the freeway was over. The return trip would take place just after noon. It would be about a four-hour commitment each day and would start in the dead of winter when road conditions can be unpredictable.

It was with much prayer, great hope, cautious anticipation, and a fleet of angels that we embarked on the "Hyperbaric Treatment, Round Two" adventure.

Nissa's former gym buddy, Sharon, headed the sign up campaign for the volunteer drivers. She had to find women who had that block of time available and orient them about the hospital routine - why Nissa was going, when she needed to be there, how long the treatment took, where to park, how to find the hyperbaric dept, etc. Sharon was a trooper with this responsibility. Week after week she managed to find the volunteer transporters who took Nissa to the hospital, waited for the treatment to be completed, and then drove her home again.

During this 3-month adventure, Nissa spent approximately 120 hours in the car with a variety of people, most of whom she didn't know. I would often ask her if she talked to the person who was driving and what they talked about. Nissa is not one to initiate conversation, nor does she have much to say once a conversation is initiated with her.

I was surprised one Sunday when someone came up to me and said, "I learned a lot about you this week." I discovered that I had been the topic of conversation that week. I was glad to hear that she was talking even if it was about me.

Everyone kept asking, "Is it doing any good?"

I always replied that we probably wouldn't know for while. I was secretly nervous that we were going through a lot of bother and expense, and inconveniencing a lot of willing drivers, only to discover that it was a wild goose chase. The nice doctor at the local hospital may have been right, that the first round of results were only a coincidence; but we had to try. Even a small improvement in her recovery could significantly change the quality of her life. We had to try.

One day shortly after the treatments were completed, I was struggling with what to do with the children's bedrooms. Nissa received nothing from the family home or division of property for the children, so their rooms had been put together with a variety of mismatched pieces of furniture. The final outcome looked like a second-hand store.

I wanted to make their rooms more functional and a little more attractive. There was a large, white, heavy, old dresser that had been passed down through our family for years in one of the rooms. The drawers were heavy and often caught as you tried to open and close them. I didn't like it and wanted to get rid of it, but thought Nissa may have some sentimental attachment to it. She had lost so much already that the few things she had became precious to her.

"Hey, I think we should get rid of that dresser." I launched into it very directly and just hoped it didn't hit a nerve.

"Oh ya do, huh?" she said in a voice that both challenged my position and stopped me dead in my tracks. Something about her voice was different. Something about her face was different and something else was different that I couldn't quite put my finger on. I replayed the interaction in my mind several times.

"Did you raise your eyebrow at me?" I finally asked.

In the old days, before the stroke, she had what we called "the evil eye" where she raised just one eyebrow when she was mad or emotional. If the eyebrow ever came up, you know you were in trouble.

"Try to raise your eyebrow. I think you just gave me the eye."

Well, that just cracked her up and she spent the next few minutes laughing. The interaction however, continued to bother me until I finally sorted it out several days later.

It wasn't that she challenged me. I've always encouraged that as part of her recovery. I've wanted her to grow more confident in her thoughts and decisions as she progressed back into her new life. It was how she challenged me that struck me so hard.

For the previous 5 years, I had grieved her loss. It felt like the sister I knew was gone and a new person had emerged. Not that anything was wrong with the new person; it just wasn't the old person. Nissa said she felt like her old self but I couldn't see it. Much of her facial tone was gone, so she didn't look the same. Her face was usually expressionless. Her voice was not the same either. I don't even remember what she used to sound like any more. And her personality felt lost to me.

What I finally realized about that day was that I had seen a glimpse of the old Nissa for just a moment. Her tone of voice, slight raise of the eyebrow, and the challenge that said, "I might not go along with this one."

"She's back!" The words came with a flash of insight. "But how could that be after all this time?" I wondered. Maybe I was just imagining it.

I reflected back several months earlier to when we were first thinking about trying hyperbaric treatment again. Since then, she had graduated from a platform, four-point walking cane to a single point cane indicating that her balance was better. She now walks with a more normal gait, steadier, a little faster, and with less concentration. She can even chew gum and walk at the same time, but still stops to talk.

A call came one day from her attorney. He wanted to meet with her. I usually went along to translate because he had a hard time understanding her and always had a list of assignments for us to write down and complete before the next contact. This time, I would be out of town. She felt confident about going alone and did. The two communicated just fine. She got her assignments and completed them without any assistance.

One morning, while on an early walk, I was reflecting on the changes and the feeling that she was more present than before. The thought came to me, "It's time to let her go."

As I reflected on "letting her go" a wave of calm washed over me. She's ready to be fully in charge of her life again and it's time for me to move from the passenger seat to the back seat. That felt right as I rehearsed it in my mind.

In the weeks that followed, there were episodes of independence that were fun for her. I marveled at how incredibly intuitive she is with her children. She is even able to raise her voice to get their attention. Before the treatment she had to blow a whistle to get their attention because she wasn't able to raise her voice. Her life with the children seemed to be moving in a more normal direction.

From a distance, the changes are likely imperceptible, but up close where I am, they are pivotal, tangible, and unmistakable. I had expected and hoped for other changes but am thrilled to have her more present, more whole, and more her. I have wondered if it was the 120 hours of socialization or the saturated oxygen, or both, that created the changes, but don't really care. I just know that I have a warm, satisfied feeling about this portion of the journey.

CHAPTER 28

Six Weeks

Five and a half years, and a trip or two to court later, Nissa finally had some real time with her children. Her baby was now nearly six years old and had never had alone time with her mother or had the opportunity to know what it was like to live with her. Every other weekend and a week vacation once a year is really artificial time, kind of like having grandparents visit. It is not living together and sharing the day-to-day journey.

Nissa was granted six weeks with her children in the summer of 2007. I was anxious to see what it would be like for them to really be together for the first time since the stroke. I wondered if Nissa would be able to keep up with them, if the house would look like a combat zone when I got home from work, and if they would get homesick for their other home.

The days started as typical summer days. Everyone was still in bed when I left for work. At first, I called home often to see how things were going. Every day I received the same assurance from Nissa and the girls. Everyone was eating breakfast, chores were getting done, and everyone was finding things to keep them entertained.

One day I arrived home to see my laundry room full of stuff and three busy little bodies. Nissa was sitting in the middle of the room and looked like a hooker who had been on a three-day drinking binge or something.

"Geri, you're next!" One of the girls grabbed me by the arm and walked me to a chair. I was still staring at Nissa. Her hair had been crimped in places, and curled in other places, and she had an assortment of clips and bows scattered all over her head. She had a thick layer of eye shadow on and a healthy stripe of blush across her cheeks. Her finger nails were done in a multiple color pattern that was quite eye catching.

"I'm next for what?" I asked, a little skeptical.

"Well, I'm going to do your hair. Then you will go over there and she will do your make-up and then she will do your nails. We're playing beauty shop today and mom has been our only customer. We need more customers so you are next." Three eager beauticians looked at me with pleading eyes.

"Can I eat dinner first?" I thought maybe that would be a slick way to get out of it, but they were on to me.

"Nope. We need you to be a customer first, and then you can eat dinner." I think they may have learned that technique from me so I was trapped.

"Okay, but I'm not looking for a total makeover." I glanced at Nissa and smiled.

"Just a little sprucing up, got it?" I said it in a way that they knew I was teasing them.

They giggled, plopped me down in the first chair, and went to work on my transformation. They were excited to have a second customer and I was glad that I didn't have to go anywhere that night.

Another evening as I returned home from work, I made it through the door leading from the garage to the house when I caught wind that the kitchen had been seized for a project.

"Geri, here is a coupon for you. You can use it when you order dinner tonight." The matter-of-fact voice announced as a small piece of paper was slipped into my hand.

"And, don't come into the kitchen until I tell you that you can." The young voice was serious and commanding.

"Okay," I obediently answered and then looked down at the paper.

"50 cents off" was hand written across the top.

The next line read, "Peach pancakes."

"So, I get 50 cents off if I order pancakes tonight?" I called as she walked away.

She turned and smiled one of those big genuine smiles and answered, "Yup."

The next thing I knew, she had found me in my bedroom and presented me with another piece of paper. This time it was a standard-size piece of copy paper that had been folded in half. Across the top the word "Menu" had been written.

I opened it up to see a list of food items carefully handwritten with a price off to the side. She watched as I carefully studied it.

"So, I can order any of these items for dinner tonight?" I asked.

"Yeah, but you have a coupon for peach pancakes."

I took that as a hint of some kind, but decided to clarify.

"So I could order anything on the menu but it would be better if I used my coupon and ordered peach pancakes?"

A look of relief came over her face as she answered, "Yes."

"Can I order right now? I'm hungry." I asked just to make sure that I understood the intended program.

"Yeah, do you want peach pancakes?" she eagerly asked.

"Sure. Do I have time to change my clothes?"

"Yeah, I'll call you when they're ready. You need to sit at the round table and tell your waitress what you want to drink. Okay?"

"So I'll have a waitress?" I asked.

Another big smile accompanied the last "yeah" as she bounced down the stairs and into the kitchen.

That night we played restaurant and were treated to a wonderfully prepared menu of breakfast foods. I thoroughly enjoyed watching them try on their new roles of chef, waitress, and bus boy.

At the end of the evening, I suggested that they hire a dishwasher type of employee since the clean-up end of the operation was not well manned. They, of course, suggested that I would be the perfect person for that job.

The six weeks passed quickly. For me they were dotted with moments of absolute delight as I watched the children just be who they are. They love the barn, the animals, the trees, the garden, the irrigation ditch, the field, the pool, and transforming parts of the house into occupations. They bring our home to life with their joyful noises and intimate connections to every aspect of where we live.

Nissa was able to keep up with the children. She generally looked a little tired by evening, but was usually in the kitchen working on dinner when I got home from work. She was great at planning meals and snacks and organizing activities. She spent hours outside, just watching them play and playing with them. Her disability did not hinder her at all in caring for them. This is what she lived for and why she chose to stay here. It was wonderful to see her able to fulfill her dreams, even if only for six weeks.

CHAPTER 29

Quantum Healing and the Slow Dance

It has been six years since the stroke and I am still searching for "the next step" on the journey. Traditional medicine is always advancing, but we have to wait for the advances to be sanctioned and then try to figure out how to pay for it.

Botox was one of those adventures. We were familiar with the medical use because of a shot Nissa was given when she discharged from the Intensive Care Unit. The doctor said it may stop the muscles on the left side of her neck from involuntarily contracting every few minutes. Botox is a derivative of the bacteria that causes botulism. Botulism causes paralysis in muscles. Botox is a sterile form of the bacteria that also causes paralysis of muscles.

Our second round with Botox came about after Nissa's leg brace had worn out. When we went to a prosthetic dealer, we were told that we needed a prescription to replace the brace. We scheduled an appointment with the Outpatient Rehabilitation department at the hospital where she had been inpatient for several months. We hoped to meet with the Rehab doctor that had cared for her when she was inpatient, but were given an appointment with his new partner who was handling the outpatient crowd.

The doctor was young, energetic, and optimistic. He suggested that a Botox injection may stop the spasticity in her left leg that is mostly paralyzed. She can move her thigh muscle just enough to lift her leg a little, but the motion creates spasticity in her left foot and toes. He theorized that loosening that muscle would allow her to walk less like Frankenstein (my word, his word was technical but I can't remember it). The downside was that it would take two injections, the injections were over one thousand dollars a piece, insurance may not pay for them, and it may not work.

We decided not to pursue the experiment unless insurance would pay for it. We were surprised to hear that it would be covered by insurance, so we scheduled the first injection. I was afraid to send her on the Paratransit for the treatment because you never know how long you will be at a doctor's office to confidently schedule a ride home, and if the injection took effect right away, she may not be able to safely get on and off the bus.

So I took time off work and accompanied her to the appointment. The injection took effect slowly and remained in effect for several days, we think. The result was that she couldn't keep her balance and fell frequently. It loosened something up alright, but she struggled to find stability with the looseness. She did physical therapy for two weeks following the injection, but there were no visible gains; so the second injection was not pursued. The doctor said that sometimes people develop immunity to the Botox so it ends up being like an immunization.

The young rehab doctor had no other new technologies or medical tricks, so we got the prescription we came for to begin with, updated her brace, and decided we would have to wait for stem cell research to mature and survive the ethical debates currently underway.

With traditional medicine on hold, I continued to look in the world of non-traditional medicine. I was wandering through a bookstore one day, looking for a birthday present for someone, when I got distracted by an aisle that had books about healing on it.

A book titled, "Quantum Healing, Exploring the Frontiers of Mind/Body Medicine," by Deepak Chopra jumped out at me. I thumbed through it enough to see that it would be interesting to me.

I am fascinated by the mind/body/spirit connection. The concept that we are a body of energy and that injury and disease are disruptions in our natural energy circuits makes sense to me. Correcting the energy circuits allows the body to heal itself. I also like the basic premise that the body has intelligence and knows how to heal itself given the correct tools to do so.

This book talked about research proving that the long-held belief that brain injury is permanent was not correct. Nerve cells can sprout new growth and brain cells will accept tissue from other organs to facilitate healing. As doctors begin to question old beliefs and introduce new possibilities, new realities come into existence.

Dr. Chopra is intent on proving that the mind's healing power is a science in its own right. He talks about consciousness as one of the factors that creates a mind/body shift. He explains that objective reality and subjective reality are tightly bound together. "When the mind shifts, the body cannot help but follow." (pg 178)

I got halfway through the book when I was broadsided. I don't know why I was talking about it at work, but I mentioned that I had tried to find the book "Slow Dance" years ago when this first happened, but couldn't locate it.

It was still odd to me that I would have a memory of a talk show that I had seen fifteen to twenty years ago about a woman who had a stroke and could still remember the name of the book that she had written. I can see the same movie twice, a year apart, and barely remember that I've seen the movie before. The fact that this memory had come back to me was amazing.

One of my young, technically-savvy co-workers overheard me and immediately got on the Internet. Within a few minutes she announced, "Amazon.com has 7 copies, all under twenty dollars."

"You are kidding?" I responded.

I couldn't believe my ears. I looked everywhere, including the Internet, just a few years before. But then a few years is a long time in the technical world and things had changed.

When I got home that night I logged on to Amazon.com and bought a copy of the book. A week later it came in the mail. It was stamped "public library" on one end and "no longer property of" on the other end. The seller put a personal note in the book stating that it was her first book sale through Amazon. I wondered if she was a librarian making extra money on the side selling books her library was disposing of. It was my first purchase from a secondhand internet bookstore, so it was a first for both of us.

I set "Quantum Healing" aside and dove into "Slow Dance." Diving for me is reading a few pages each night before I fall asleep, so it is a slow process to get through a book. I was totally captured by this book and got through it in a few weeks (that's fast for me).

I was drawn to how alike this woman's story was to Nissa's. Their pre-stroke lives were similar - both young (for a stroke) and healthy (no medical conditions that generally precede a stroke). The stroke was big enough to produce total paralysis and she too had been reduced to eye blinks for communication. Her family and doctors feared that she would die, but were willing to hope for the best and stayed the course through the long, slow, uncertain recovery process.

Bonnie authored her own recovery story in "Slow Dance, A Story of Stroke, Love and Disability." She told a story that paralleled Nissa's story in many ways, but from a first-person perspective. She explained things that Nissa could not, shared insights that I had hungered for, and verbalized feelings and thoughts that were validating to me. I felt like there was at least one other person on the planet that understood our journey and that felt good.

There was one stark contrast in their stories. Bonnie's husband stayed by her side. He got past the paralysis and then the drooling, incontinence, choking, and inconvenience of her dependence on caretakers. He reached through her disability and stayed intimately connected to the woman he loved.

He told her that marrying her was the best decision he had ever made and he wasn't about to change his mind about that decision. He was incredibly loyal even though his wife had changed so dramatically in her physical and emotional presentation. He rode the waves of adversity and adapted his life to make it more compatible with her circumstances. He was an amazing man whose advocacy promoted his wife's recovery. It was truly a love story.

"Quantum Healing" had put me in a hopeful mood again in regards to recovery. I had visions of functional movement in her partially-paralyzed left hand or walking with no cane at all (something she did a little of around the house already). I was excited to be on the recovery journey again.

The last part of "Slow Dance" dealt with the world of disability. Bonnie reached a point where she believed that it was as good as it was going to get. She then stepped into the world of being disabled and became a spokesperson in that arena. She accepted her disability and lived with it.

I still vacillated between the world of "believing" and the world of "today's reality," but often sat on the fence between them. These two books came into my life at the same time and intensified the conflict I felt. The questions were everpresent: When do we quit pushing forward and accept where we are at? When do we say it is enough?

A part of me absolutely believes that she can heal. I've seen miracles (physical realities that I do not understand) and have no reason to doubt that more will follow. On the other hand, I have embraced that she is disabled and realize that her world as a disabled person, and my world as her primary support system, will always have an uphill slope.

The times I climb off the fence, I am usually on the recovery side of the equation and want to keep pushing forward. Nissa goes through waves of resting and waves of pushing forward also. I suspect that she and I will be looking for the next step and walking that uphill road until her dream of running again comes true.

In the mean time, we keep just keep believing ... and watching the latest news on stem cell research.

CHAPTER 30

It Inspires Me

A few years ago I visited a cemetery from the 1800s where many children were buried. I was moved by how they recounted their days with the child. The inscriptions read 2 years, 5 months, and 11 days, like every day was precious and needed to be counted.

The finalization of Nissa's divorce felt much like a death, but what I felt like recounting was how long it took for the death to be final. It was exactly 4 years, 11 months and 18 days from when the divorce papers were first filed (on Nissa's wedding anniversary) to the date they were signed by a judge.

Several times in that nearly five-year period, Nissa was lead to believe that the divorce would be finalized soon, only to have six more months go by with no mention of it. Attorneys were talking to each other because another "order to show cause" against the "other party" was in motion and a court date had been set.

"Maybe you could ask your attorney to find out what happened to your divorce since he's talking to the other attorney anyway." I made suggestions like that from time to time.

It was always something. "The divorce papers are incomplete. We are waiting for a signature. We need this or we need that. The divorce papers have been filed. The papers are lost." Always something that seemed silly, like someone really didn't want the divorce to be final. It didn't seem like it should be that complicated. People get divorced every day, sometimes very quickly.

A feeling that something was different this time kept nagging me. I hated when that happened because it lead to me feeling compelled to get involved again. There seemed to be a few more pieces in place this time even though no one could locate the divorce papers anywhere. His attorney said she filed them months ago, but they had never made it to the judge for signature and so appeared to be lost again.

"I wonder if you are divorced and just don't know it?" I posed the question to Nissa.

Nissa just looked at me and shrugged her shoulders.

"Wanna find out?" I asked carefully.

I really thought it would be better for her to know than to have any surprises originating from the "other party" at the upcoming court hearing.

"Sure," she answered in a "whatever" tone of voice, as if she didn't believe it was possible.

Nissa gave me the case number on her divorce papers so I could do some research. One of Nissa's friends suggested that we go online and look it up. We tried that but did not have success.

I called the court information line one night after hours and punched in the case number. An automated voice came on the line and said, "The matter was signed by Judge so and so on July 31, 2008." It was not the judge involved in the case so I didn't recognize the name. It was now mid August, so something had been signed two weeks before.

The next day I called the court and patiently waited through all of the telephone options on the automated system, pushing the buttons that I hoped would eventually lead to a live person. I was delighted when a live voice came on the other end of the line and didn't even mind that she was a little cranky.

I gave her the case number and asked if she could tell me the outcome of the case. She began to read notes from the last hearing.

I interrupted her and asked, "Can you tell me if they are divorced?"

She was quiet for a minute or two as she continued to read silently.

"Yes, they are divorced. It was signed by the judge on July 31, 2008."

"Really!" I exclaimed in a surprised tone.

"They don't even know it and the attorneys think the papers are lost. How are you supposed to find out you are divorced? Doesn't the court notify the filing attorney?"

"You don't know unless you keep checking. The court doesn't just send things out unless someone requests and pays for it." She emphasized the "pays for it" part.

"Wow," was all I could say.

"Is that all?" The voice on the other end of the line asked.

"Yes, thank you." I replied and hung up the phone.

I immediately called Nissa at home to let her know.

"You're divorced! You've been divorced for two weeks. How about that?" I blurted out.

We had talked the night before about the message I heard on the automated system, so it was not a complete surprise.

"Hmmm" was her only response.

As the next few days passed, I waited for an emotional reaction from Nissa, but that is not what occurred. Instead, I saw a confidence slowly emerge. She felt a little more "normal" to me and less "disabled." Her dress, her hair style, her make-up, and her routine were still the same, but how she wore them all was just a little different. She seemed a little more like herself to me, like she had been set free. It was subtle, but there was clearly an internal shift that had visible markers on the surface.

It was about two weeks later that a fat envelope from her attorney arrived in the mail. Nissa was curious and quickly opened it. Surprised again, it was the divorce decree. Reading through it, she discovered things that were not in the original papers she signed so many months before.

It was odd to be notified by mail, a month after the divorce was actually signed, that she was divorced. It was also odd to read a document that had her signature at the end of it that contained things she had never seen before. The decree had some interesting additions! But then, odd seemed to be the norm in this case so it should not have been surprising.

The following week I received a phone call shortly after I had crawled in bed for the night. It was Nissa. Nissa often goes to the temple with a neighbor one evening a week. Afterwards, they stop for ice cream and usually arrive home about the time I retire to my bedroom upstairs.

When I answered the phone, Nissa attempted to speak but instead broke into laughter. It is sometimes hard to tell if she is laughing or crying so I listened carefully. She was definitely laughing.

It took several tries for her to get out a few simple words.

"I got hit on tonight."

She then had to repeat it multiple times before I could understand her.

"You got hit on tonight?" I asked, as if I couldn't believe what I was saying.

"What do you mean you got hit on tonight?" I was sure that I did not understand what I just heard.

"A man at the temple asked me for my phone number and I gave it to him."

The question "what kind of man" came to mind, but didn't seem polite to say out loud; so I was silent until I could come up with another way to ask the question. I was suspicious of predatory intentions even if she had met him in a religious setting. And her disability had attracted some unusual characters in the past.

"How old was he?" That seemed a little less judgmental.

"He looked like he was about my age," she replied.

The next question that popped into my mind was, "What's wrong with him?" but again, I elected to do some editing before I opened my mouth. After all, why would something have to be wrong with him?

I honestly believe there is a man out there somewhere that will see past her disability, get to know her, and develop a relationship with who she is on the inside rather than just reacting to what they see on the outside. I figured this man could only be reacting to what he saw on the outside, so I was suspicious and wanted to know what he was up to.

"So," I started cautiously, "is he a goober like the one that followed you out to the car last month?"

I decided to do the humor thing to see if it would help get to the point. I felt badly about calling the last interested party a derogatory name, but I knew she would understand.

"No, he actually looked pretty normal," she answered after she stopped laughing. She seemed truly joyful about this little surprise in her life.

"Well, congratulations! The universe must have put the word out that you are free again."

The synchronicity of this happening right after her divorce being finalized totally amazed me. It was exciting, interesting, and certainly laced with anticipation.

It was about a week later when Shylee (Nissa's first child who was now twelve years old), Nissa, and I were in the backyard just hanging out in the gazebo when Nissa's phone rang.

Shylee grabbed the phone and said "Hello?"

She had a puzzled look on her face as she handed the phone to her mother and said, "It's for you."

She watched her mother talk on the phone for just a minute and then turned to me.

"Does my mother have a boyfriend?" she asked, with an unusual intensity in her voice.

I wondered what she was thinking and if I should tell her anything or wait until Nissa got off the phone and let her talk to Shylee.

I looked over at Nissa and caught her attention with my eyes. Nissa silently mouthed the words, "It's Mark" so I would know who she was talking to. Shylee watched the exchange, but was still looking for an answer. It looked like Nissa would be on the phone for a while, so I decided to give Shylee some kind of answer.

"Do you know that your parents are finally divorced?" I wanted to lay the foundation of why her mother might be talking to a man on the phone.

Shylee looked like I had just slapped her. Her eyes went wide and almost had a look of horror in them as she shook her head "no."

"Great!" I thought. "Nobody has told her anything!"

"Your parents were officially divorced about a month ago. Your mom didn't even know until about two weeks ago. But now that she is divorced, it is okay for her to be with other men." I paused for a minute to see if she was following me.

"The man your mom is talking to on the phone asked for her phone number last week. And now, it looks like he is giving her a call."

The shocked look on Shylee's face slowly melted into a delighted smile.

"My mom has a boyfriend!" She seemed as excited about that thought as she had been shocked about the divorce.

"I don't know about that, but she does have a boy calling her on the phone," I replied with some caution in my voice.

We then both turned our attention to Nissa and eavesdropped on the rest of the conversation, which mostly consisted of "okay, okay, okay."

Nissa hit the "end" button on her phone and then announced, "He's going to call me later. We might get together on Friday."

"My mom has a boyfriend and she's going on a date! Cool!" Shylee was clearly excited.

I just smiled and wondered where this little turn of events would lead. I was again amazed at the synchronicity of events, that Mark would call when Nissa was with Shylee, and that Shylee would feel compelled to grab the phone and answer it.

Nissa continued to talk with Mark on the phone every other day or so and eventually agreed to meet him in downtown Provo on Friday night. She was not sure what the plan was from there. Tim and I dropped her off a little early and went to a restaurant across the street. After I ordered, I went back out to check on her. She was still waiting for him. I walked across the street to talk to her.

Looking at my watch I said, "Give him a few more minutes. If he doesn't show up, give him a call. If he doesn't answer his phone, we are in the second booth on the right as you go in that restaurant right over there" and pointed to where Tim and I had ordered dinner.

Tim and I chatted about nothing while we ate dinner. I was pretty distracted wondering if Nissa was okay and wondering who the mysterious Mark really was. We finished dinner and left the restaurant. Our car was parked right across from where Mark was supposed to pick her up. She was gone, so we assumed he had come after all. We were to be her ride home so needed to be available, but didn't know where she had gone or what she was doing. We decided to stay in town and do some errands.

Errands, ice cream, shopping, and several hours went by. It was getting late. Restaurants were closing, the downtown theaters had patrons pouring out the doors, and anything they may have been doing downtown would be coming to a close. Nissa's phone was turned off so we couldn't reach her. We had not been able to prearrange a place or time to pick her back up because she didn't know what the plan was for the date.

There was a point where I became officially worried and started to think through possibilities. If I had to report her missing, I have no idea who she is with except for a first name. If she had her phone and it worked, surely she would let me know what the plan was for getting her home. She was usually tired by this time of the night and would certainly want to be coming home by now. Where could they have possibly gone that would take them over 3 hours? And how long did I wait before really panicking?

My phone finally did ring. Nissa was calm and confident. They were in a restaurant a few blocks from where we had dropped her off and would be coming out soon.

About 15 minutes went by before they made it to the car. Nissa was smiling and Mark was quite conversant. He seemed happy to push her in her wheelchair and did not seem the least bit put off by her condition. He watched her get into the car and then helped load her wheelchair. He then told her goodbye and headed off down the street.

"So what did you guys do?" I really wondered how they managed to occupy that much time downtown.

"We just went out to eat."

"You've been at the restaurant for two and a half hours?" I had a hard time believing that.

"Yeah," she said with a giggle.

"What did you do at a restaurant for two and half hours?" I was still having a hard time with the whole idea.

"We just talked." She was glowing from the back seat and seemed to have enjoyed her time with Mark.

"You don't talk that much. You've never talked that much. What did you talk about for two and half hours?" I was giving her a hard time now.

"Lots of things, everything, nothing." She was laughing now.

"I can't believe you talked for two and a half hours. That's crazy. You don't talk that much. Nobody would believe you talked for that long. Why was your phone off? I was about to report you as a missing person." I was teasing her again.

"I kept getting calls so I turned my phone off." She had received several calls from her ex-husband's phone number and didn't want her date interrupted by him.

As I unloaded her wheelchair when we got home, I noticed a white napkin slide off the seat and on to the garage floor. I assumed it was trash, but didn't want to find a trash can right then so just picked it up and put it in the back of the car, figuring that I could throw it away the next day.

I then went upstairs and got ready for bed. Just as I was snuggling in for the night the phone rang. It was Nissa. She generally calls me on the phone if I am upstairs because it is too hard for her to make it upstairs and she can't yell loud enough for me to hear her.

"Did you find a napkin when you loaded my wheelchair into the car?" she asked.

I hesitated, not knowing if she was talking about what I thought had been trash.

"Ummm, yeah, I think so," I answered.

"There is something on it that I wanted to show you."

I had a hard time imaging anything I would want to see on a napkin or that she would want to show me on a napkin, but figured it was important if she called me to tell me about it.

"Should I go look for it?" I asked to see if it was really important to her.

"Yeah," she answered.

Normally she wouldn't want to put me out or have me go out of my way for her, so the fact that she thought it was important enough for me to get out of bed for perked my curiosity.

I turned on lights and made my way down the stairs and through the house to the garage. I flipped open the back of the car and located the napkin. I was glad that I hadn't rumpled it up or thrown it away. It was folded in half and had been tucked under her leg in the wheelchair.

I unfolded it and noticed that there was some writing on it. I moved to a spot in the garage where there was sufficient light to read the writing.

It started with "Man I hope you understand where I come from in this note." The opening line made me nervous. I wondered who had written it.

I took a deep breath and then went on. I was really curious now.

"When I meet someone like you and see how you are so happy, it inspires me to be a better person. Thank you."

I read it again and then again. As I read, a picture came into my mind of Nissa and Mark talking about "everything and nothing" and enjoying each other's company as the note's author watched them.

I went back into the house and to Nissa's room.

"Who gave you this note?" I asked.

"The waiter brought it to me and said that someone had asked him to deliver it to me. I don't know who wrote it," she explained.

I read it again and imagined whomever wrote it thinking to them self, "If someone handicapped can enjoy their life, then I have no excuse to not enjoy my life," or something like that.

The words "it inspires me" resonated as I read the note again. I smiled at Nissa and said "cool" as I laid the napkin on her night stand and left her room.

"It inspires me" was still echoing in my mind as I climbed up the stairs to my room. My thoughts rolled into questions, "Is that what this is all about? Is her mission to inspire others?" I said a quick prayer of thanks for the brave man who dared to share his feelings on a napkin that night, and then drifted into my own world of thoughts and feelings about her.

I concluded that I agree with the napkin man.

It inspires me too.

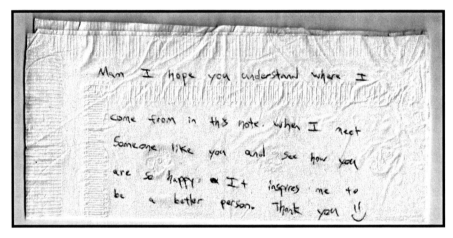

The "it inspires me" message on napkin.

Nissa in 2008; 7 years post stroke and still recovering.

Our family in 2008
Left to right   Bottom row: Jesse, Shaura, Carli
Top row: Teena, Shylee, McKenzie, Tim, Geri and Nissa

Epilogue

It has been exactly seven years this month since the stroke changed the tides in all of our lives. It is an anniversary we no longer dread, nor one that brings grief. Our lives are full and we all continue to grow and change.

Nissa still progresses in her recovery, although in very small increments. I have had dreams where I have seen her completely whole again, but for now she is still paralyzed on one side. The paralysis seems to be less of an obstacle as time goes by. She continues to inspire those around her and has a gift of bringing out the best in others.

The girls are all very close to their mother and enjoy the time that they are able to be with her. Carli has been able to have some private time with her "mama" and has developed a strong relationship with her. It seems like only yesterday that we started on this journey and now the girls are half grown. I know that it will seem just like another blink and they will be grown and gone.

Acknowledgments

Thank you Nissa, for allowing me to walk with you on this incredible journey. It has filled my world with the serenity and joy that comes when you emerge from dark shadows into warmth and light. Your smile is sunshine to me.

Thank you Tim, for being an anchor during this stormy time. You have been incredibly supportive and patient with me and Nissa and the children. You have a houseful of adoring women in your life that you put up with very well. We love you for being a man that we can count on.

Jesse and Teena, thanks for being my back-up when I was spread too thin to cover all of the bases. You two are an important part of our family menagerie and have been the fill in the cracks that kept me together. And Jesse... thanks for finding Shaura and bringing her light into our lives.

Thanks to all of the family members, especially Mom, who pray for us, support us, and cheer us on.

Thank you Lee, for suggesting that I write a story and for the coaching and mentoring as I kept writing stories.

Thanks to Lisa and Bruce and everyone else that helped me to fine tune what I was trying to say in the book.

Thank you Trish, for taking me away so that I had quiet times and places to concentrate on writing.

Thanks to Agate Cove Inn and Cousin Roger for providing me with the perfect hide away to finish the book.

Thanks to Scott Spjut for editing. I did make some last-minute changes, but hopefully didn't mess up your good work.

And thanks to all of the angels (mortal and immortal) who have walked with us. You have lifted, carried, rescued, encouraged, supported, and loved us when we needed you to. You are why I have the strength to keep believing.